Ninja Foodi Grill Cookbook

1000-Day Ninja Foodi Grill Cookbook for Beginners and Advanced 2021 | Tasty, Quick & Easy Recipes for Intdoor Grilling & Air Frying Perfection

Clarew Milner

© Copyright 2021 Clarew Milner - All Rights Reserved.

In no way is it legal to reproduce, duplicate, or transmit any part of this document by either electronic means or in printed format. Recording of this publication is strictly prohibited, and any storage of this material is not allowed unless with written permission from the publisher. All rights reserved.

The information provided herein is stated to be truthful and consistent, in that any liability, regarding inattention or otherwise, by any usage or abuse of any policies, processes, or directions contained within is the solitary and complete responsibility of the recipient reader. Under no circumstances will any legal liability or blame be held against the publisher for any reparation, damages, or monetary loss due to the information herein, either directly or indirectly.

Respective authors own all copyrights not held by the publisher.

Legal Notice:

This book is copyright protected. This is only for personal use. You cannot amend, distribute, sell, use, quote or paraphrase any part of the content within this book without the consent of the author or copyright owner. Legal action will be pursued if this is breached.

Disclaimer Notice:

Please note the information contained within this document is for educational and entertainment purposes only. Every attempt has been made to provide accurate, up-to-date and reliable, complete information. No warranties of any kind are expressed or implied. Readers acknowledge that the author is not engaging in the rendering of legal, financial, medical or professional advice.

By reading this document, the reader agrees that under no circumstances are we responsible for any losses, direct or indirect, which are incurred as a result of the use of information contained within this document, including, but not limited to, errors, omissions, or inaccuracies.

Table of Contents

Introduction 5
Chapter 1: The Basics of Ninja Foodi Grill 6
   What is Ninja Foodi Grill? 6
   The Ninja Foodi Grill Accessories 6
   Operating Buttons and Functions 7
   Benefits of Ninja Foodi Gill 9
   Cleaning and Maintenance 10
Chapter 2: Breakfast 12
   Delicious Baked Oatmeal 12
   Broccoli Cauliflower Bake 13
   Scalloped Potatoes 14
   Zucchini Casserole 15
   Cheese Egg Bake 16
   Crispy Breakfast Potatoes 17
   Greek Egg Muffins 18
   Greek Egg Muffins 19
   Spinach Frittata 20
   Quinoa Egg Muffins 21
Chapter 3: Poultry 22
   Marinated Grill Chicken 22
   Juicy Chicken Thighs 23
   Grill Greek Chicken 24
   Spicy Chicken Wings 25
   Grilled Chicken Breast 26
   Chicken Meatballs 27
   Baked Chicken Breast 28
   Crunchy Chicken Tenders 29
   Ranch Chicken Wings 30
   Easy Jerk Chicken Wings 31
   Sweet & Spicy Chicken Wings 32
   Herb Chicken Breast 33
   Tasty Turkey Meatballs 34
   Spinach Turkey Burger Patties 35
   Chicken Burger Patties 36

   Asian Chicken Thighs 37
   Basil Thyme Chicken Breast 38
   Meatballs 39
   Garlic Mustard Chicken 40
   Flavorful Southwest Chicken 41
Chapter 4: Beef Pork & Lamb 42
   Grilled Pork Chops 42
   Marinated Pork Chops 43
   Creole Lamb Chops 44
   Tuscan Steak 45
   Asian Lamb Chops 46
   Mexican Steak 47
   Tender & Juicy Meatballs 48
   Mini Meatloaf 49
   Tasty Steak Bites 50
   Meatballs 51
   Mustard Meatballs 52
   Spicy Pork Patties 53
   Crispy Pork Chops 54
   Herb Pork Chops 55
   Flavorful Honey Pork Chops 56
   Juicy Pork Chops 57
   Easy Pork Bites 58
   Delicious Pork Chops 59
   Simple & Tasty Pork Chops 60
   Meatballs 61
Chapter 5: Fish & Seafood 62
   Grilled Salmon Patties 62
   Lemon Garlic Salmon 63
   Flavorful Mahi Mahi 64
   Blackened Cod 65
   Spicy Shrimp 66
   Dijon Salmon Fillets 67
   Cajun Fish Fillets 68

Sweet & Spicy Salmon 69
Tasty Crab Cakes 70
Lemon Pepper Shrimp 71
Spicy Scallops 72
Baked Halibut 73
Bagel Fish Fillets 74
Delicious Tuna Steaks 75
Easy Lemon Pepper Fish Fillets 76

Chapter 6: Vegetable & Side Dishes 77
Healthy Spinach Casserole 77
Tasty Cauliflower Steaks 78
Flavorful Sweet Potatoes 79
Zucchini Spinach Casserole 80
Delicious Zucchini Sticks 81
Stuffed Peppers 82
Flavorful Baby Potatoes 83
Tasty Hasselback Potatoes 84
Spicy Brussels Sprouts 85
Mexican Potatoes 86
Zucchini Burger Patties 87
Healthy Asparagus 88
Easy Herb Mushrooms 89
Baked Carrots 90
Baked Zucchini Casserole 91

Chapter 7: Snacks & Appetizers 92
Healthy & Delicious Roasted Peas 92
Tasty Roasted Chickpeas 93
Sausage Meatballs 94
Easy Squash Fries 95
Stuffed Jalapenos 96
Roasted Nuts 97
Healthy Yuca Fries 98
Delicious Chicken Patties 99
Easy Sausage Balls 100
Flavorful Tofu Bites 101

Healthy Carrot Fries 102
Tasty Potato Nuggets 103
Cinnamon Sweet Potato Bites 104
Spicy Peanuts 105
Savory Cashew Nuts 106

Chapter 8: Dehydrate 107
Mango Slices 107
Green Apple Chips 108
Dried Raspberries 109
Avocado Chips 110
Strawberry Chips 111
Sweet Potato Chips 112
Cucumber Chips 113
Beet Chips 114
Carrot Chips 115
Dehydrated Pineapple 116
Orange Chips 117
Kiwi Chips 118
Apple Chips 119
Eggplant Slices 120
Squash Chips 121

Chapter 9: Desserts 122
Spiced Apples 122
Blueberry Muffins 123
Pound Cake 124
Choco Almond Muffins 125
Moist Brownies 126
Easy Butter Cake 127
Baked Donuts 128
Peanut Butter Muffins 129
Strawberry Cobbler 130
Lemon Muffins 131

Chapter 10: 30-Day Meal Plan 132
Conclusion 135

Introduction

Another revolutionary cooking appliance comes from Ninja Family is popularly known as Ninja Foodi Grill. These multifunctional cooking appliances not only grill your food but also air fry, roast, bake, and even dehydrate your favourite foods. The body of the appliances is made up of stainless steel and the upper domed lid is made from a plastic material. The accessories like grill grate, cooking pot, the crisper pot come with ceramic non-stick coating. It works on 1760 watts and produces a maximum 500°F to 510°F temperature while cooking your food.

The ninja grill comes with a 6-quart cooking pot capacity and 4 quarts crisper pot capacity. You can also use it as a dehydrator and it allows dehydrating 18 slices at a single cooking cycle. The digital control panel is easy to read and anyone can easily operate the appliances. You just need to select the desire cooking function and set the time and temperature settings by navigating the up and down arrow key as per recipe requirements. The ninja foodi uses rapid hot air circulation techniques to cook food faster and evenly from all the sides.

This cookbook contains tasty, healthy, and delicious recipes that come from different categories like breakfast, poultry, beef, pork & lamb, fish & seafood, vegetable & side dishes, snacks & appetizers, dehydrate, and desserts. The recipes written in this book are unique and written in an easily understandable form. All the recipes are written with their preparation and cooking time with step by step cooking instructions. The recipes written in this book are ends with their nutritional value information. The nutritional value information will help to keep track of daily calorie consumption. The book also contains 30 days meal plan. There are various cookbooks are available in the market on this topic thanks for choosing my book. I hope you love and enjoy all the recipes written in this cookbook.

Chapter 1: The Basics of Ninja Foodi Grill

What is Ninja Foodi Grill?

Ninja foodi grill is an advanced multifunctional and revolutionary indoor cooking appliance available in the market. The Ninja Foodi grill is versatile cooking appliances capable to perform 5 in 1 different cooking functions like grilling, Air crisping, Roasting, Baking, and Dehydrating your food. The pot is made with stainless steel material having 4-quart in capacity and works on 1760 watt power. The ninja foodi grill is loaded with different cooking accessories like a non-stick ceramic coated grill grate, crisper pot, cooking pot, and a cleaning brush.

The Ninja Foodi Grill uses cyclonic grilling techniques that cooks your food faster and evenly from all the sides. It rapidly circulates the superheated cyclonic air around the food and gives you crispier, fired grilled flavored food within very less time. It creates 500°F hot air to cook your food perfectly. Due to rapid hot air circulation, you never need to flip your food, you will get perfect even cooking results. The Ninja foodi grill comes with four different temperature settings low, medium, high, and max settings. These settings allow you to cook your food precisely without making smoke in your kitchen. Beyond grilling ninja foodi is capable to perform different cooking tasks. It air fry your favorite food with very less oil and fats compared with the deep-frying method and makes make your food crispy from the outside, juicy tender from the inside. You can roast your favourite chicken or meat, bake your favourite cake and cookies and dehydrate your favourite fruit, vegetable, and meat slices.

The ninja foodi is capable to cook your frozen food without defrosting. It transforms your frozen food into char grill meals within 25 minutes. The ninja foodi grill having a digital control panel system which makes it easy to operate the cooking appliance. You just need to select the appropriate cooking functions given on the control panel and set the desired time and temperature settings as per your recipe needs.

The Ninja Foodi Grill Accessories

The Ninja foodi grill is loaded with various accessories which makes your daily cooking process faster and easier. These accessories include:

- **Crisper Pot**

The crisper pot comes with a non-stick ceramic coating and used while air frying your favorite food like French fries and wings or making crispy Brussels sprout serve with a combination of grilled chicken. The crisper pot is also used to dehydrate your favorite fruit, veggies, and meat slices. While using the crisper pot always use a wooden or silicone utensil to avoid scratches over the crisper pot.

- Cooking Pot

The cooking pot is one of the main utensils of the ninja foodi grill, it is always installed while using this appliance. You can use a grill grate and crisper pot with a cooking pot. The pot comes with a non-stick ceramic coating which makes your cleaning process easy. While using other accessories like grill grate and crisper pot with cooking pot use wooden or silicone utensils to avoid scratches over the pot.

- Grill Grates

The grill grates come with a non-stick ceramic coating and are designed to heat up at 500°F rapidly while the grill circulates super-heated air into the cooking chamber. The grill grate makes char marks on your food and gives you even and fast cooking results without making too much smoke. While using the grill grate always wise wooden or silicone utensils to avoid unwanted scratches over the grill grate.

- Hood

The hood is the topmost part of your ninja foodi grill consist of heating elements with a convection fan to circulate superheated air into the cooking chamber. While you are using air crisp, roast, bake and dehydrate functions the fan speed is automatically adjusted by ninja foodi grill. The hood comes with a splatter shield which protects heating elements from splatter to avoid unwanted smoke.

- Grease collector

It is situated at the backside of the ninja foodi grill and used to collect the grease trapped by the hood. While cleaning your ninja foodi grill make sure the grease collector is empty and clean it during the cleaning process.

Operating Buttons and Functions

Operating Buttons

- Power Button

Once you plugged the power cable into the power socket using the power button to turn on the main unit. If you press the power button during the cooking cycle the current working cooking function stops and the unit goes turn off.

- **Temp**

This function is used to adjust the temperature settings while using any function over the control panel. To use this function select the desire cooking function and adjust the temperature settings by pressing the temp up and down arrow keys. When you are using grill settings the temp up and down arrow keys help you to easily navigate between low, mid, high, and max settings.

- **Time**

This function is used to adjust the time settings while using any function on the control panel. To use this function select the desire cooking function and adjust the time settings by pressing the time up and down arrow keys.

- **START/STOP button**

When you are selecting the desire function with time and temperature settings then press this button to start the cooking process. If you press this button during the cooking process the cooking process will stop.

- **STANDBY mode**

Your ninja foodi grill goes standby mode if the machine is not in the running process or if you have not made any interaction for 10 minutes with the control panel.

Functions

- **Grill**

Using this function you can grill your favorite chicken breast, meat, steaks, and more. While using this function you never need to flip your food, it makes your food crispier and also gives brown texture over your food like regular grilling. To get better results you need to preheat your ninja foodi grill for 8 minutes before placing the food. To get the best grilling results to use grilling grates while using this function.

- **Air Crisp**

This function is ideal for air frying purposes using this function you can air fry your favorite fries, chicken wings, and more. The ninja foodi grill opens from the top so it is easy to flip your fries compare to the regular air fryer. You can easily move the crisper pot place inside the ninja foodi grill. It makes your food crisper from the outside and juicy tender from the inside.

- Roast

Using this function you can tenderize your favorite meat, roast small cuts of meat, roast your favorite vegetables, and more. It gives a nice crust over your food and keeps your food tender and juicy.

- Baking

The ninja foodi cooking pot holds a large 8-inch baking pan so you can bake a cake using a ninja foodi grill. Don't except a perfect cake the final product comes out is brown, tender with the crust.

- Dehydrating

This function is used to dehydrate your favorite fruit, vegetable, and meat slices. The ninja foodi grill capable to hold 18 slices at a time and an apple takes about 7 hours to dehydrate completely.

Benefits of Ninja Foodi Gill

The Ninja Foodi Grill loaded with various benefits some of the benefits as give as follows:

1. **Compact in size**

The ninja foodi grill is compact and easily fits on the kitchen countertop without taking too much space. You can easily transport and move the ninja foodi grill.

2. **Easy to operate**

The ninja foodi grill comes with big size digital control panel system. The different functions are given on the panel you just need to select the proper function and adjust the time and temperature settings as per your recipe needs.

3. **Multi-functional appliances**

Most of the indoor cooking appliances comes with multi-functional cooking operations. The ninja foodi grill is not just using for grilling purposes but also use to air fry, baking, roasting, and dehydrating your food. You never need to purchase separate appliances to perform these single cooking operations.

4. Healthy cooking

The ninja foodi grill air fries your food using very little fats and oils. It saves 75 to 80% of oil compared to the traditional deep frying method. Less fat and oil means healthy cooking results.

5. Cooks your food faster and evenly

The ninja foodi grill works on rapid cyclonic air circulation technology in which superheated air near about 500°F to 510 °F is circulated into the cooking chamber with the help of a convection fan. It helps to cook your food faster and gives you even cooking results after every cooking cycle.

6. Smokeless grilling

This is another benefit of using an indoor grill it doesn't create smokes like regular outdoor grilling. If you do not have an outdoor area then the ninja foodi grill is one of the best indoor grilling options available to cook your food without filling your kitchen with smoke.

7. Crisp and brown result

The ninja foodi grill cooks your food by circulating hot air around the food this will create delicious and mouth-watering flavors during the browning process. It not only add flavors and the browning effect it also makes your food crunchy.

8. Easy to clean

All the accessories like grill grate, crisper pot, the cooking pot comes with non-stick ceramic coatings. So they create less mess and you can easily clean all these accessories into the dishwasher.

Cleaning and Maintenance

It is recommended that to clean your ninja foodi grill after each use. The following step by step cleaning instructions will help you to clean your ninja foodi grill easily.

1. Before starting the cleaning process unplug the ninja foodi grill from the power socket and let it be cool down at room temperature. For faster cooling keep the hood of the ninja foodi grill open.
2. Now remove the accessories like grill grate, crispier pot, cooking pot, and splatter shield for cleaning. All these accessories are dishwasher safe so you can easily clean them into the dishwasher.
3. You can also hand wash these accessories with the help of a cleaning brush for getting better cleaning results. You can also use the end of the cleaning brush as a scraper to remove derbies.
4. If still there is any splatter or residue over the grill grate, splatter shield or any other part then soak these accessories into soapy water overnight and then clean it with a cleaning brush.
5. Use a soft damp cloth to clean the main unit from the outside.
6. Before placing the accessories at their original position make sure all these accessories are dry thoroughly.
7. Now your ninja foodi grill is ready for next use.

Chapter 2: Breakfast

Delicious Baked Oatmeal

Preparation Time: 10 minutes
Cooking Time: 40 minutes
Serve: 8

Ingredients:

- 2 eggs
- 2 cups old-fashioned oats
- 1/4 cup almonds, sliced
- 1/4 cup dried cherries
- 1/4 cup dried blueberries
- 1 tsp ground cinnamon
- 1/4 cup canola oil
- 3/4 cup brown sugar
- 3 cups milk
- 1 tsp salt

Directions:

1. In a mixing bowl, whisk eggs with milk, sugar, oil, cinnamon, and salt.
2. Stir in oats, cherries, and blueberries.
3. Transfer oat mixture into the greased baking dish. Cover the dish and place in the refrigerator for overnight.
4. Place the cooking pot in the unit.
5. Select bake mode set the temperature to 350 F and set the time to 40 minutes. Press start to begin preheating.
6. Remove baking dish from refrigerator while the unit is heating. Stir oatmeal and sprinkle with sliced almonds.
7. Once the unit is preheated then place the baking dish in the cooking pot. Close with a lid and cook for 40 minutes.
8. Serve and enjoy.

Nutritional Value (Amount per Serving):

- Calories 271
- Fat 12.6 g
- Carbohydrates 33.6 g
- Sugar 18.2 g
- Protein 7.7 g
- Cholesterol 48 mg

Broccoli Cauliflower Bake

Preparation Time: 10 minutes
Cooking Time: 50 minutes
Serve: 8

Ingredients:

- 3 eggs, lightly beaten
- 12 oz broccoli florets
- 12 oz cauliflower florets
- 8 oz Velveeta cheese, cubed
- 1/2 cup milk
- 2 tbsp flour
- 1 small onion, chopped
- 2 tbsp butter
- 1/4 tsp salt

Directions:

1. Melt butter in a saucepan over medium-high heat.
2. Add onion and sauté for 2-3 minutes. Stir in flour until well blended.
3. Add milk and whisk well. Bring to boil, stir continuously, and cook for 1-2 minutes.
4. Stir in salt and cheese until cheese is melted.
5. Remove saucepan from heat. Slowly whisk in eggs. Add broccoli and cauliflower and stir well. Transfer mixture into the greased baking dish.
6. Place the cooking pot in the unit.
7. Select bake mode set the temperature to 325 F and set the time to 50 minutes. Press start to begin preheating.
8. Once the unit is preheated then place the baking dish in the cooking pot. Close with a lid and cook for 50 minutes.
9. Serve and enjoy.

Nutritional Value (Amount per Serving):

- Calories 173
- Fat 11.1 g
- Carbohydrates 11.3 g
- Sugar 5 g
- Protein 10 g
- Cholesterol 91 mg

Scalloped Potatoes

Preparation Time: 10 minutes
Cooking Time: 50 minutes
Serve: 6

Ingredients:

- 4 cups potatoes, peeled & sliced
- 1 cup onions, sliced
- ½ cup cheddar cheese, shredded
- 1 ½ cups milk
- 3 tbsp flour
- 2 tbsp butter
- ¼ tsp pepper
- 1 tsp salt

Directions:

1. Melt butter in a saucepan over medium heat. Add flour, pepper, and salt and stir until smooth. Slowly whisk in milk. Bring to boil, stir continuously for 2 minutes.
2. Remove saucepan from heat. Add cheese and stir until cheese is melted.
3. Arrange half potato slices in a greased baking dish then layer with ½ cup onion and half cheese sauce. Repeat layers.
4. Place the cooking pot in the unit.
5. Select bake mode set the temperature to 350 F and set the time to 50 minutes. Press start to begin preheating.
6. Once the unit is preheated then place the baking dish in the cooking pot. Close with a lid and cook for 50 minutes.
7. Serve and enjoy.

Nutritional Value (Amount per Serving):

- Calories 194
- Fat 8.4 g
- Carbohydrates 23.7 g
- Sugar 4.8 g
- Protein 6.7 g
- Cholesterol 25 mg

Zucchini Casserole

Preparation Time: 10 minutes
Cooking Time: 25 minutes
Serve: 6

Ingredients:

- 2 eggs, lightly beaten
- 1 cup Colby-Monterey jack cheese, shredded
- 1 ½ cups crackers, crushed
- 1 onion, chopped
- 7 cups zucchini, chopped
- ¼ cup butter
- ¼ tsp pepper
- 1 tsp salt

Directions:

1. Melt 2 tablespoons of butter in a pan over medium heat.
2. Add onion and zucchini and cook for 10-12 minutes or until tender. Remove pan from heat and let it cool.
3. Melt remaining butter. In a small bowl, mix crushed crackers and melted butter.
4. In a mixing bowl, mix together eggs, cheese, and sautéed zucchini and onion, pepper, and salt.
5. Transfer zucchini mixture into the greased baking dish. Sprinkle with crushed crackers.
6. Place the cooking pot in the unit.
7. Select bake mode set the temperature to 350 F and set the time to 25 minutes. Press start to begin preheating.
8. Once the unit is preheated then place the baking dish in the cooking pot. Close with a lid and cook for 25 minutes.
9. Serve and enjoy.

Nutritional Value (Amount per Serving):

- Calories 269
- Fat 19.4 g
- Carbohydrates 16.3 g
- Sugar 3.6 g
- Protein 9.4 g
- Cholesterol 93 mg

Cheese Egg Bake

Preparation Time: 10 minutes
Cooking Time: 25 minutes
Serve: 4

Ingredients:

- 8 eggs, lightly beaten
- 1 cup cheddar cheese, shredded
- ¼ tsp pepper
- ¼ cup tomatillo salsa
- 2 tbsp butter, melted
- ¼ cup milk
- 1 cup ham, chopped into 1-inch pieces
- ½ tsp salt

Directions:

1. In a bowl, whisk eggs with salsa, butter, milk, ham, pepper, and salt.
2. Pour egg mixture into the greased baking dish and top with cheese.
3. Place the cooking pot in the unit.
4. Select bake mode set the temperature to 375 F and set the time to 25 minutes. Press start to begin preheating.
5. Once the unit is preheated then place the baking dish in the cooking pot. Close with a lid and cook for 25 minutes.
6. Serve and enjoy.

Nutritional Value (Amount per Serving):

- Calories 365
- Fat 27.1 g
- Carbohydrates 3.6 g
- Sugar 1.5 g
- Protein 24.4 g
- Cholesterol 393 mg

Crispy Breakfast Potatoes

Preparation Time: 10 minutes
Cooking Time: 23 minutes
Serve: 6

Ingredients:

- 2 lbs potatoes, peel and cut into ½-inch cubes
- 1 tbsp parsley, minced
- ½ tsp onion powder
- ½ tsp paprika
- ½ tsp garlic powder
- ¼ tsp pepper
- 3 tbsp olive oil
- 1 tsp kosher salt

Directions:

1. In a large mixing bowl, add potatoes and remaining ingredients and mix well.
2. Transfer potatoes into the baking dish.
3. Place the cooking pot in the unit.
4. Select bake mode set the temperature to 400 F and set the time to 23 minutes. Press start to begin preheating.
5. Once the unit is preheated then place the baking dish in the cooking pot. Close with a lid and cook for 23 minutes. Stir potatoes halfway through.
6. Serve and enjoy.

Nutritional Value (Amount per Serving):

- Calories 167
- Fat 7.2 g
- Carbohydrates 24.3 g
- Sugar 1.9 g
- Protein 2.7 g
- Cholesterol 0 mg

Greek Egg Muffins

Preparation Time: 10 minutes
Cooking Time: 20 minutes
Serve: 6

Ingredients:

- 6 eggs
- 1/4 cup fresh basil, chopped
- 1/3 cup sun-dried tomatoes, chopped
- 1/3 cup feta cheese, crumbled
- Pepper
- Salt

Directions:

1. In a bowl, whisk eggs with tomatoes, cheese, basil, pepper, and salt.
2. Pour egg mixture into the 6 silicone muffin molds.
3. Place the cooking pot in the unit.
4. Select bake mode set the temperature to 375 F and set the time to 20 minutes. Press start to begin preheating.
5. Once the unit is preheated then place muffin molds in the cooking pot. Close with a lid and cook for 20 minutes.
6. Serve and enjoy.

Nutritional Value (Amount per Serving):

- Calories 87
- Fat 6.2 g
- Carbohydrates 1.1 g
- Sugar 0.9 g
- Protein 6.8 g
- Cholesterol 171 mg

Greek Egg Muffins

Preparation Time: 10 minutes
Cooking Time: 25 minutes
Serve: 6

Ingredients:

- 1 cup egg whites
- 1 roasted red pepper, chopped
- 1 cup baby spinach, chopped
- 1 green onions, chopped
- 2 tbsp feta cheese, crumbled
- 6 olives, pitted & chopped
- Pepper
- Salt

Directions:

1. Divide olives, pepper, and spinach in 6 silicone muffin molds.
2. In a bowl, whisk egg whites with green onions, feta cheese, pepper, and salt.
3. Pour egg mixture into the prepared muffin molds.
4. Place the cooking pot in the unit.
5. Select bake mode set the temperature to 350 F and set the time to 25 minutes. Press start to begin preheating.
6. Once the unit is preheated then place muffin molds in the cooking pot. Close with a lid and cook for 25 minutes.
7. Serve and enjoy.

Nutritional Value (Amount per Serving):

- Calories 40
- Fat 1.3 g
- Carbohydrates 1.8 g
- Sugar 1 g
- Protein 5.2 g
- Cholesterol 3 mg

Spinach Frittata

Preparation Time: 10 minutes
Cooking Time: 20 minutes
Serve: 6

Ingredients:

- 6 eggs
- 1/2 cup frozen spinach, defrosted & drained
- 1/2 tsp garlic powder
- 1 tsp oregano
- 1/4 cup milk
- 1/4 cup feta cheese, crumbled
- 1/2 cup olives, chopped
- 1/2 cup tomatoes, diced
- 1/4 tsp salt

Directions:

1. In a bowl, whisk eggs with oregano, garlic powder, milk, pepper, and salt until well combined.
2. Add olives, feta, tomatoes, and spinach and stir well.
3. Pour egg mixture into the greased baking dish.
4. Place the cooking pot in the unit.
5. Select bake mode set the temperature to 400 F and set the time to 20 minutes. Press start to begin preheating.
6. Once the unit is preheated then place the baking dish in the cooking pot. Close with a lid and cook for 20 minutes.
7. Serve and enjoy.

Nutritional Value (Amount per Serving):

- Calories 102
- Fat 7.2 g
- Carbohydrates 2.8 g
- Sugar 1.5 g
- Protein 7.1 g
- Cholesterol 170 mg

Quinoa Egg Muffins

Preparation Time: 10 minutes
Cooking Time: 25 minutes
Serve: 6

Ingredients:

- 3 eggs
- 1 1/2 cups mixed vegetables, cooked
- 1/2 cup feta cheese, crumbled
- 1 cup egg whites
- 1/2 cup fresh parsley, chopped
- 1 tbsp onion powder
- 1 cup cooked quinoa
- Pepper
- Salt

Directions:

1. In a bowl, whisk egg whites and eggs. Add remaining ingredients and stir well.
2. Pour egg mixture into the 6 silicone muffin molds.
3. Place the cooking pot in the unit.
4. Select bake mode set the temperature to 350 F and set the time to 25 minutes. Press start to begin preheating.
5. Once the unit is preheated then place muffin molds in the cooking pot. Close with a lid and cook for 25 minutes.
6. Serve and enjoy.

Nutritional Value (Amount per Serving):

- Calories 218
- Fat 6.8 g
- Carbohydrates 24.8 g
- Sugar 1.4 g
- Protein 14.1 g
- Cholesterol 93 mg

Chapter 3: Poultry

Marinated Grill Chicken

Preparation Time: 10 minutes
Cooking Time: 12 minutes
Serve: 6

Ingredients:

- 6 chicken breasts
- 2 tsp garlic powder
- 1/2 tsp black pepper
- 2 tbsp Dijon mustard
- 2 tsp dried rosemary
- 3/4 cup brown sugar
- 2 tbsp fresh lemon juice
- 1/4 cup Worcestershire sauce
- 1/4 cup soy sauce
- 1/2 cup balsamic vinegar
- 1/2 cup olive oil
- 2 tsp salt

Directions:

1. Add all ingredients except chicken into the large mixing bowl and mix until well combined.
2. Add chicken into the zip-lock bag then pour marinade over chicken. Seal bag shake well and place in the refrigerator for overnight.
3. Place the cooking pot in the unit then place the grill plate in the pot.
4. Select grill mode set the temperature to medium and set the time to 8 minutes. Press start to begin preheating.
5. Once the unit is preheated then place marinated chicken on the grill plate. Close with a lid and cook for 6 minutes.
6. After 6 minutes flip the chicken, cover with a lid, and cook for 6 minutes.
7. Serve and enjoy.

Nutritional Value (Amount per Serving):

- Calories 520
- Fat 28 g
- Carbohydrates 22.2 g
- Sugar 20.2 g
- Protein 43.4 g
- Cholesterol 130 mg

Juicy Chicken Thighs

Preparation Time: 10 minutes
Cooking Time: 14 minutes
Serve: 2

Ingredients:

- 1 lb chicken thighs, boneless & skinless
- For marinade:
- 1/2 tsp garlic, minced
- 1/2 tsp dried rosemary
- 1/2 tsp lemon pepper seasoning
- 1/2 tbsp soy sauce
- 1/2 tbsp Dijon mustard
- 1/2 tbsp balsamic vinegar
- 1/2 tbsp brown sugar
- 1 1/2 tbsp olive oil

Directions:

1. Add all marinade ingredients into the zip-lock bag and mix well.
2. Add chicken thighs into the marinade. Seal bag, shake well and place in the refrigerator for overnight.
3. Place the cooking pot in the unit then place the grill plate in the pot.
4. Select grill mode set the temperature to medium and set the time to 8 minutes. Press start to begin preheating.
5. Once the unit is preheated then place marinated chicken on the grill plate. Close with a lid and cook for 7 minutes.
6. After 7 minutes flip the chicken, cover with a lid, and cook for 7 minutes or until the internal temperature of the chicken reaches to 165 F.
7. Serve and enjoy.

Nutritional Value (Amount per Serving):

- Calories 538
- Fat 27.5 g
- Carbohydrates 3.5 g
- Sugar 2.3 g
- Protein 66.1 g
- Cholesterol 202 mg

Grill Greek Chicken

Preparation Time: 10 minutes
Cooking Time: 10 minutes
Serve: 4

Ingredients:

- 4 chicken breasts, boneless & skinless
- 1/2 tsp dried rosemary
- 1/2 tsp dried thyme
- 1/2 tsp dried basil
- 2 tsp dried oregano
- 1 tbsp garlic, minced
- 1/3 cup fresh lemon juice
- 1 tbsp lemon zest
- 1/3 cup olive oil
- Pepper
- Salt

Directions:

1. Add all ingredients except chicken into the zip-lock bag and mix well.
2. Add chicken into the zip-lock bag. Seal bag, shake well and place in the refrigerator for overnight.
3. Place the cooking pot in the unit then place the grill plate in the pot.
4. Select grill mode set the temperature to high and set the time to 6 minutes. Press start to begin preheating.
5. Once the unit is preheated then place marinated chicken on the grill plate. Close with a lid and cook for 5 minutes.
6. After 5 minutes flip the chicken, cover with a lid, and cook for 5 minutes or until the internal temperature of the chicken reaches to 165 F.
7. Serve and enjoy.

Nutritional Value (Amount per Serving):

- Calories 434
- Fat 27.9 g
- Carbohydrates 2.1 g
- Sugar 0.6 g
- Protein 42.7 g
- Cholesterol 130 mg

Spicy Chicken Wings

Preparation Time: 10 minutes
Cooking Time: 45 minutes
Serve: 6

Ingredients:

- 3 lbs chicken wings, pat dry with a paper towel
- 2 tsp baking powder
- 1/2 tsp pepper
- 3 tbsp butter
- 1 cup Frank's red hot sauce
- 1/2 tsp garlic powder
- 1/2 tsp salt

Directions:

1. In a large bowl, mix baking powder, garlic powder, pepper, and salt. Add chicken wings and toss well.
2. Place the cooking pot in the unit.
3. Select bake mode set the temperature to 450 F and set the time to 25 minutes. Press start to begin preheating.
4. Once the unit is preheated then place chicken wings in the cooking pot. Close with a lid and cook for 25 minutes. Flip chicken wings and cook for 20 minutes more.
5. Melt butter in a pan over medium heat. Transfer melted butter and hot sauce in a large bowl and mix well.
6. Add chicken wings in the sauce and toss well to coat.
7. Serve and enjoy.

Nutritional Value (Amount per Serving):

- Calories 489
- Fat 22.7 g
- Carbohydrates 1.7 g
- Sugar 0.5 g
- Protein 65.9 g
- Cholesterol 217 mg

Grilled Chicken Breast

Preparation Time: 10 minutes
Cooking Time: 20 minutes
Serve: 6

Ingredients:

- 1 1/2 lbs chicken breast
- 2 lime zest
- 2 lime juice
- 1/4 cup olive oil
- 2 garlic cloves, minced
- 1 tsp tomato paste
- 1/2 tsp onion powder
- 1 tsp ground cumin
- 1 tsp smoked paprika
- 2 chipotle peppers
- Salt

Directions:

1. Add all ingredients except chicken into the blender and blend until well combined.
2. Add chicken into the zip-lock bag and pour the blended mixture over the chicken. Seal bag shake well to coat the chicken.
3. Allow the chicken to marinate for overnight.
4. Place the cooking pot in the unit then place the grill plate in the pot.
5. Select grill mode set the temperature to medium and set the time to 8 minutes. Press start to begin preheating.
6. Once the unit is preheated then place marinated chicken on the grill plate. Close with a lid and cook for 10 minutes.
7. After 10 minutes flip the chicken, cover with a lid, and cook for 10 minutes or until the internal temperature of the chicken reaches to 165 F.
8. Serve and enjoy.

Nutritional Value (Amount per Serving):

- Calories 216
- Fat 11.4 g
- Carbohydrates 3.8 g
- Sugar 1.3 g
- Protein 24.6 g
- Cholesterol 73 mg

Chicken Meatballs

Preparation Time: 10 minutes
Cooking Time: 25 minutes
Serve: 6

Ingredients:

- 1 lb ground chicken
- 1/4 cup almond flour
- 1/2 lime zest
- 2 spring onions, chopped
- 1/4 cup cilantro, chopped
- 1 tsp ginger garlic paste
- 1 tsp chili, minced
- 1 tbsp fish sauce
- Pepper
- Salt

Directions:

1. Add all ingredients into the large bowl and mix until well combined.
2. Make 30 balls from the meat mixture.
3. Place the cooking pot in the unit.
4. Select bake mode set the temperature to 390 F and set the time to 25 minutes. Press start to begin preheating.
5. Once the unit is preheated then place meatballs in the cooking pot. Close with a lid and cook for 25 minutes.
6. Serve and enjoy.

Nutritional Value (Amount per Serving):

- Calories 158
- Fat 6.4 g
- Carbohydrates 1.4 g
- Sugar 0.3 g
- Protein 22.6 g
- Cholesterol 67 mg

Baked Chicken Breast

Preparation Time: 10 minutes
Cooking Time: 20 minutes
Serve: 3

Ingredients:

- 3 chicken breasts, skinless & boneless
- 1/2 tsp ground black pepper
- 1/2 tsp garlic powder
- 1/2 tsp paprika
- 1/2 tsp Italian seasoning
- 2 tbsp olive oil
- 1/2 tsp salt

Directions:

1. For the brine: Add 2 tablespoons of salt and warm water in a large bowl and stir until salt is dissolved. Add chicken breasts in brine and let it sit for 30 minutes.
2. Remove chicken from brine and pat dry with a paper towel.
3. Brush chicken breasts with oil.
4. In a small bowl, mix garlic powder paprika, Italian seasoning, pepper, and salt.
5. Sprinkle seasoning mixture over chicken breasts.
6. Place the cooking pot in the unit.
7. Select bake mode set the temperature to 450 F and set the time to 20 minutes. Press start to begin preheating.
8. Once the unit is preheated then place chicken in the cooking pot. Close with a lid and cook for 20 minutes.
9. Serve and enjoy.

Nutritional Value (Amount per Serving):

- Calories 363
- Fat 20.4 g
- Carbohydrates 0.9 g
- Sugar 0.2 g
- Protein 42.4 g
- Cholesterol 130 mg

Crunchy Chicken Tenders

Preparation Time: 10 minutes
Cooking Time: 15 minutes
Serve: 6

Ingredients:

- 1 egg
- 1 lb chicken breast, boneless & cut into pieces
- 1 tsp onion powder
- 1 tsp garlic powder
- 1 1/2 tsp paprika
- 1/4 cup ground flaxseed meal
- 1/2 cup parmesan cheese, grated
- 1 1/2 cups almond flour
- Pepper
- Salt

Directions:

1. Season chicken tenders with pepper and salt.
2. In a shallow dish, mix parmesan cheese, almond flour, onion powder, garlic powder, flaxseed meal, pepper, and salt. Set aside.
3. Add egg in a separate bowl and whisk well.
4. Dip each chicken piece in egg then coat with cheese mixture.
5. Place the cooking pot in the unit.
6. Select bake mode set the temperature to 350 F and set the time to 15 minutes. Press start to begin preheating.
7. Once the unit is preheated then place coated chicken pieces in the cooking pot. Close with a lid and cook for 15 minutes.
8. Serve and enjoy.

Nutritional Value (Amount per Serving):

- Calories 185
- Fat 9 g
- Carbohydrates 4.5 g
- Sugar 0.6 g
- Protein 22.1 g
- Cholesterol 81 mg

Ranch Chicken Wings

Preparation Time: 10 minutes
Cooking Time: 25 minutes
Serve: 2

Ingredients:

- 1 lb chicken wings
- 2 tbsp butter, melted
- 1 1/2 tbsp ranch seasoning
- 1 tbsp garlic, minced

Directions:

1. In a large bowl, mix together butter, garlic, and ranch seasoning.
2. Add chicken wings and toss to coat. Cover bowl and place in the refrigerator for overnight.
3. Place the cooking pot in the unit then place the crisper basket in the pot.
4. Select air crisp mode set the temperature to 360 F and set the time to 25 minutes. Press start to begin preheating.
5. Once the unit is preheated then place chicken wings in the crisper basket. Close with a lid and cook. Turn chicken wings halfway through.
6. Serve and enjoy.

Nutritional Value (Amount per Serving):

- Calories 561
- Fat 28.4 g
- Carbohydrates 1.4 g
- Sugar 0.1 g
- Protein 66 g
- Cholesterol 232 mg

Easy Jerk Chicken Wings

Preparation Time: 10 minutes
Cooking Time: 20 minutes
Serve: 2

Ingredients:

- 1 lb chicken wings
- 1 tsp butter, melted
- 1 tbsp jerk seasoning
- 1 tbsp cornstarch
- Pepper
- Salt

Directions:

1. In a bowl, add chicken wings. Add remaining ingredients on top of chicken wings and toss to coat.
2. Place the cooking pot in the unit then place the crisper basket in the pot.
3. Select air crisp mode set the temperature to 380 F and set the time to 20 minutes. Press start to begin preheating.
4. Once the unit is preheated then place chicken wings in the crisper basket. Close with a lid and cook. Turn chicken wings halfway through.
5. Serve and enjoy.

Nutritional Value (Amount per Serving):

- Calories 463
- Fat 18.7 g
- Carbohydrates 3.7 g
- Sugar 0 g
- Protein 65.7 g
- Cholesterol 207 mg

Sweet & Spicy Chicken Wings

Preparation Time: 10 minutes
Cooking Time: 30 minutes
Serve: 4

Ingredients:

- 1 lb chicken wings
- 2 tbsp sriracha sauce
- 1/4 cup honey
- 1 tbsp butter
- 1 1/2 tbsp soy sauce
- Pepper
- Salt

Directions:

1. Season chicken wings with pepper and salt.
2. Place the cooking pot in the unit then place the crisper basket in the pot.
3. Select air crisp mode set the temperature to 360 F and set the time to 30 minutes. Press start to begin preheating.
4. Once the unit is preheated then place chicken wings in the crisper basket. Close with a lid and cook. Turn chicken wings halfway through.
5. Meanwhile, add butter, soy sauce, sriracha sauce, and honey in a saucepan and cook for 3 minutes.
6. Add chicken wings into the bowl. Pour sauce over chicken wings and toss until well coated.
7. Serve and enjoy.

Nutritional Value (Amount per Serving):

- Calories 359
- Fat 16.3 g
- Carbohydrates 18.4 g
- Sugar 18 g
- Protein 33.3 g
- Cholesterol 114 mg

Herb Chicken Breast

Preparation Time: 10 minutes
Cooking Time: 25 minutes
Serve: 4

Ingredients:

- 4 chicken breasts, skinless & boneless
- 1 tbsp olive oil
- For rub:
- 1 tsp oregano
- 1 tsp thyme
- 1 tsp parsley
- 1 tsp onion powder
- 1 tsp basil
- Pepper
- Salt

Directions:

1. Brush chicken breast with olive oil.
2. In a small bowl, mix together all rub ingredients and rub all over chicken breasts.
3. Place the cooking pot in the unit.
4. Select bake mode set the temperature to 390 F and set the time to 25 minutes. Press start to begin preheating.
5. Once the unit is preheated then place chicken breasts in the cooking pot. Close with a lid and cook for 25 minutes. Turn chicken halfway through.
6. Serve and enjoy.

Nutritional Value (Amount per Serving):

- Calories 312
- Fat 14.4 g
- Carbohydrates 0.9 g
- Sugar 0.2 g
- Protein 42.4 g
- Cholesterol 130 mg

Tasty Turkey Meatballs

Preparation Time: 10 minutes
Cooking Time: 20 minutes
Serve: 4

Ingredients:

- 1 egg, lightly beaten
- 1 lb ground turkey
- 1 tsp garlic, minced
- 1/4 cup basil, chopped
- 3 tbsp scallions, chopped
- 1/2 cup almond flour
- 1/2 tsp red pepper, crushed
- 1 tbsp lemongrass, chopped
- 1 1/2 tbsp fish sauce

Directions:

1. Add all ingredients into a large bowl and mix until well combined.
2. Make small balls from the meat mixture.
3. Place the cooking pot in the unit.
4. Select bake mode set the temperature to 380 F and set the time to 20 minutes. Press start to begin preheating.
5. Once the unit is preheated then place meatballs in the cooking pot. Close with a lid and cook for 20 minutes. Turn meatballs halfway through.
6. Serve and enjoy.

Nutritional Value (Amount per Serving):

- Calories 268
- Fat 15.4 g
- Carbohydrates 3.1 g
- Sugar 1.3 g
- Protein 33.8 g
- Cholesterol 157 mg

Spinach Turkey Burger Patties

Preparation Time: 10 minutes
Cooking Time: 22 minutes
Serve: 4

Ingredients:

- 1 lb ground turkey
- 1 tsp Italian seasoning
- 4 oz feta cheese, crumbled
- 1 1/4 cup spinach, chopped
- 1 tbsp olive oil
- 1 tbsp garlic paste
- Pepper
- Salt

Directions:

1. Add all ingredients into the mixing bowl and mix until well combined.
2. Make four equal shapes of patties from the mixture.
3. Place the cooking pot in the unit then place the crisper basket in the pot.
4. Select air crisp mode set the temperature to 390 F and set the time to 22 minutes. Press start to begin preheating.
5. Once the unit is preheated then place patties in the crisper basket. Close with a lid and cook. Turn patties halfway through.
6. Serve and enjoy.

Nutritional Value (Amount per Serving):

- Calories 335
- Fat 22.4 g
- Carbohydrates 2.3 g
- Sugar 1.3 g
- Protein 35.5 g
- Cholesterol 142 mg

Chicken Burger Patties

Preparation Time: 10 minutes
Cooking Time: 18 minutes
Serve: 4

Ingredients:

- 1 lb ground chicken
- 1 tbsp oregano
- 1/2 tsp garlic powder
- 1.5 oz mozzarella cheese, shredded
- 1/4 tsp onion powder
- 3.5 oz breadcrumbs
- Pepper
- Salt

Directions:

1. Add all ingredients into the mixing bowl and mix until well combined.
2. Make four equal shapes of patties from the meat mixture.
3. Place the cooking pot in the unit then place the crisper basket in the pot.
4. Select air crisp mode set the temperature to 360 F and set the time to 18 minutes. Press start to begin preheating.
5. Once the unit is preheated then place patties in the crisper basket. Close with a lid and cook. Turn patties halfway through.
6. Serve and enjoy.

Nutritional Value (Amount per Serving):

- Calories 349
- Fat 11.7 g
- Carbohydrates 19.4 g
- Sugar 1.7 g
- Protein 39.3 g
- Cholesterol 107 mg

Asian Chicken Thighs

Preparation Time: 10 minutes
Cooking Time: 20 minutes
Serve: 4

Ingredients:

- 1 lb chicken thighs
- 1 tbsp soy sauce
- 1/4 cup creamy peanut butter
- 1/2 cup water
- 1 tsp ginger, minced
- 1 tbsp sriracha sauce
- 1 tsp garlic, minced
- 2 tbsp lime juice
- 2 tbsp sweet chili sauce
- 1/2 tsp salt

Directions:

1. In a large bowl, whisk together peanut butter, sriracha sauce, ginger, water, soy sauce, sweet chili sauce, lime juice, garlic, and salt.
2. Add chicken into the bowl and coat well. Cover and place in the fridge for overnight.
3. Place the cooking pot in the unit then place the crisper basket in the pot.
4. Select air crisp mode set the temperature to 350 F and set the time to 20 minutes. Press start to begin preheating.
5. Once the unit is preheated then remove chicken from marinade and place in the crisper basket. Close with a lid and cook for 20 minutes. Turn chicken halfway through.
6. Serve and enjoy.

Nutritional Value (Amount per Serving):

- Calories 360
- Fat 19.1 g
- Carbohydrates 9.1 g
- Sugar 5.2 g
- Protein 37.3 g
- Cholesterol 103 mg

Basil Thyme Chicken Breast

Preparation Time: 10 minutes
Cooking Time: 10 minutes
Serve: 2

Ingredients:

- 2 chicken breasts, boneless and skinless
- 1 tsp dried oregano
- 1 tsp dried basil
- 2 tsp garlic, minced
- 1 tsp dried thyme
- Pepper
- Salt

Directions:

1. In a small bowl, mix together garlic, thyme, oregano, basil, pepper, and salt and rub all over the chicken.
2. Place the cooking pot in the unit then place the crisper basket in the pot.
3. Select air crisp mode set the temperature to 400 F and set the time to 10 minutes. Press start to begin preheating.
4. Once the unit is preheated then place chicken in the crisper basket. Close with a lid and cook for 10 minutes.
5. Serve and enjoy.

Nutritional Value (Amount per Serving):

- Calories 285
- Fat 11 g
- Carbohydrates 1.8 g
- Sugar 0.1 g
- Protein 42.6 g
- Cholesterol 130 mg

Meatballs

Preparation Time: 10 minutes
Cooking Time: 10 minutes
Serve: 4

Ingredients:

- 1 egg, lightly beaten
- 1 lb ground turkey
- 1/4 cup fresh parsley, chopped
- 1 tbsp soy sauce
- 1/2 cup breadcrumbs
- Pepper
- Salt

Directions:

1. Add all ingredients into the large bowl and mix until well combined.
2. Make small balls from the meat mixture.
3. Place the cooking pot in the unit then place the crisper basket in the pot.
4. Select air crisp mode set the temperature to 400 F and set the time to 10 minutes. Press start to begin preheating.
5. Once the unit is preheated then place meatballs in the crisper basket. Close with a lid and cook for 10 minutes. Turn meatballs halfway through.
6. Serve and enjoy.

Nutritional Value (Amount per Serving):

- Calories 294
- Fat 14.3 g
- Carbohydrates 10.4 g
- Sugar 1 g
- Protein 34.6 g
- Cholesterol 157 mg

Garlic Mustard Chicken

Preparation Time: 10 minutes
Cooking Time: 20 minutes
Serve: 4

Ingredients:

- 1 lb chicken tenders
- 1/2 cup whole grain mustard
- 1/2 tsp paprika
- 2 tbsp fresh tarragon, chopped
- 1/2 tsp pepper
- 1 tsp garlic, minced
- 1/2 oz fresh lemon juice
- 1/4 tsp kosher salt

Directions:

1. Add all ingredients except chicken to the large bowl and mix well.
2. Add chicken and stir until well coated.
3. Place the cooking pot in the unit then place the crisper basket in the pot.
4. Select air crisp mode set the temperature to 380 F and set the time to 20 minutes. Press start to begin preheating.
5. Once the unit is preheated then place chicken tenders in the crisper basket. Close with a lid and cook for 20 minutes. Turn chicken halfway through.
6. Serve and enjoy.

Nutritional Value (Amount per Serving):

- Calories 241
- Fat 9.5 g
- Carbohydrates 3.1 g
- Sugar 0.1 g
- Protein 33.2 g
- Cholesterol 101 mg

Flavorful Southwest Chicken

Preparation Time: 10 minutes
Cooking Time: 25 minutes
Serve: 2

Ingredients:

- 1/2 lb chicken breasts, skinless and boneless
- 1/4 tsp cumin
- 1 tbsp lime juice
- 1/8 tsp garlic powder
- 1/8 tsp onion powder
- 1/8 tsp chili powder
- 1/2 tbsp olive oil
- 1/8 tsp salt

Directions:

1. Add all ingredients into the zip-lock bag. Seal bag, shake well, and place in the fridge for 1 hour.
2. Place the cooking pot in the unit then place the crisper basket in the pot.
3. Select air crisp mode set the temperature to 400 F and set the time to 25 minutes. Press start to begin preheating.
4. Once the unit is preheated then place chicken in the crisper basket. Close with a lid and cook. Turn chicken halfway through.
5. Serve and enjoy.

Nutritional Value (Amount per Serving):

- Calories 254
- Fat 12 g
- Carbohydrates 2.3 g
- Sugar 0.5 g
- Protein 33 g
- Cholesterol 101 mg

Chapter 4: Beef Pork & Lamb

Grilled Pork Chops

Preparation Time: 10 minutes
Cooking Time: 10 minutes
Serve: 4

Ingredients:

- 4 pork chops, boneless
- 1 tbsp olive oil
- For seasoning:
- 1/4 tsp dried basil
- 1/4 tsp dried onion, minced
- 1/4 tsp dried parsley
- 1/4 tsp garlic powder
- Salt

Directions:

1. In a small bowl, mix together all seasoning ingredients.
2. Brush pork chops with oil and rub with seasoning.
3. Place the cooking pot in the unit then place the grill plate in the pot.
4. Select grill mode set the temperature to high and set the time to 8 minutes. Press start to begin preheating.
5. Once the unit is preheated then place pork chops on the grill plate. Close with a lid and cook for 5 minutes.
6. Turn pork chops and cook for 5 minutes more or until the internal temperature of pork chops reaches to 145 F.
7. Serve and enjoy.

Nutritional Value (Amount per Serving):

- Calories 287
- Fat 23.4 g
- Carbohydrates 0.2 g
- Sugar 0.1 g
- Protein 18 g
- Cholesterol 69 mg

Marinated Pork Chops

Preparation Time: 10 minutes
Cooking Time: 10 minutes
Serve: 2

Ingredients:

- 2 pork chops
- For marinade:
- 1 tbsp brown sugar
- 1/4 cup soy sauce
- 1/4 cup lemon juice
- 1/3 cup olive oil
- 1/2 tsp oregano
- 1 tsp onion powder
- Pepper

Directions:

1. Add marinade ingredients into the zip-lock bag and mix well.
2. Add pork chops into the zip-lock bag. Seal bag, shake well and place in the refrigerator for overnight.
3. Place the cooking pot in the unit then place the grill plate in the pot.
4. Select grill mode set the temperature to high and set the time to 8 minutes. Press start to begin preheating.
5. Once the unit is preheated then place marinated pork chops on the grill plate. Close with a lid and cook for 5 minutes.
6. After 5 minutes flip pork chops, cover with a lid and cook for 5 minutes.
7. Serve and enjoy.

Nutritional Value (Amount per Serving):

- Calories 591
- Fat 53.8 g
- Carbohydrates 8.7 g
- Sugar 6 g
- Protein 20.4 g
- Cholesterol 69 mg

Creole Lamb Chops

Preparation Time: 10 minutes
Cooking Time: 10 minutes
Serve: 6

Ingredients:

- 6 lamb chops
- 1 tsp ground white pepper
- 1 tsp thyme, minced
- 1 tsp Creole seasoning
- 1/2 tsp garlic, minced
- 1 tbsp fresh rosemary, minced
- Pepper
- Salt

Directions:

1. Season lamb chops with pepper and salt and set aside.
2. In a small bowl, mix white pepper, thyme, Creole seasoning, garlic, and rosemary and rub over lamb chops.
3. Place the cooking pot in the unit then place the grill plate in the pot.
4. Select grill mode set the temperature to high and set the time to 8 minutes. Press start to begin preheating.
5. Once the unit is preheated then place lamb chops on the grill plate. Close with a lid and cook for 5 minutes.
6. After 5 minutes flip lamb chops, cover with a lid, and cook for 5 minutes.
7. Serve and enjoy.

Nutritional Value (Amount per Serving):

- Calories 612
- Fat 24.1 g
- Carbohydrates 0.8 g
- Sugar 0 g
- Protein 91.9 g
- Cholesterol 294 mg

Tuscan Steak

Preparation Time: 10 minutes
Cooking Time: 14 minutes
Serve: 4

Ingredients:

- 1 1/2 lbs porterhouse steaks
- 3 tbsp olive oil
- 2 tbsp fresh rosemary, chopped
- 1/2 tsp pepper
- 2 tsp kosher salt

Directions:

1. In a small bowl, mix oil, rosemary, pepper, and salt.
2. Brush steaks with oil mixture.
3. Place the cooking pot in the unit then place the grill plate in the pot.
4. Select grill mode set the temperature to high and set the time to 8 minutes. Press start to begin preheating.
5. Once the unit is preheated then place steaks on the grill plate. Close with a lid and cook for 7 minutes.
6. After 7 minutes flip steaks, cover with a lid, and cook for 7 minutes.
7. Serve and enjoy.

Nutritional Value (Amount per Serving):

- Calories 441
- Fat 27.2 g
- Carbohydrates 1.2 g
- Sugar 0 g
- Protein 46.4 g
- Cholesterol 99 mg

Asian Lamb Chops

Preparation Time: 10 minutes
Cooking Time: 10 minutes
Serve: 6

Ingredients:

- 12 lamb chops
- For seasoning:
- 1/2 tsp ground coriander
- 1 tbsp chili powder
- 1 tbsp brown sugar
- 1 tbsp turmeric powder
- 1 tsp kosher salt

Directions:

1. In a small bowl, mix all seasoning ingredients and rub all over lamb chops.
2. Place the cooking pot in the unit then place the grill plate in the pot.
3. Select grill mode set the temperature to high and set the time to 8 minutes. Press start to begin preheating.
4. Once the unit is preheated then place lamb chops on the grill plate. Close with a lid and cook for 5 minutes.
5. After 5 minutes flip lamb chops, cover with a lid, and cook for 5 minutes.
6. Serve and enjoy.

Nutritional Value (Amount per Serving):

- Calories 654
- Fat 52.3 g
- Carbohydrates 2.9 g
- Sugar 1.6 g
- Protein 38.2 g
- Cholesterol 160 mg

Mexican Steak

Preparation Time: 10 minutes
Cooking Time: 10 minutes
Serve: 4

Ingredients:

- 1 1/2 lbs skirt steak
- 1/2 tsp pepper
- 1/2 cup pickled jalapenos, sliced
- 2 tbsp olive oil
- 2 garlic cloves, chopped
- 1 onion, chopped
- 1/3 cup lime juice
- 1 cup cilantro, chopped
- 1/2 tsp salt

Directions:

1. Add cilantro, lime juice, garlic, oil, jalapenos, pepper, and salt to the blender and blend until smooth.
2. Add steak into the mixing bowl. Pour blended mixture over steak and coat well and let it marinate for 30 minutes.
3. Place the cooking pot in the unit then place the grill plate in the pot.
4. Select grill mode set the temperature to high and set the time to 8 minutes. Press start to begin preheating.
5. Once the unit is preheated then place marinated steak on the grill plate. Close with a lid and cook for 5 minutes.
6. After 5 minutes flip the steak, cover with a lid, and cook for 5 minutes.
7. Serve and enjoy.

Nutritional Value (Amount per Serving):

- Calories 427
- Fat 24.4 g
- Carbohydrates 3.8 g
- Sugar 1.3 g
- Protein 45.9 g
- Cholesterol 100 mg

Tender & Juicy Meatballs

Preparation Time: 10 minutes
Cooking Time: 12 minutes
Serve: 4

Ingredients:

- 1 egg
- 1 1/2 lbs ground beef
- 1/4 tsp pepper
- 1/2 tsp onion powder
- 1/2 tsp Italian seasoning
- 1 tbsp parmesan cheese, grated
- 2 tbsp parsley, chopped
- 2 tbsp milk
- 1/3 cup breadcrumbs
- 1/2 tsp salt

Directions:

1. Add all ingredients into the large bowl and mix until well combined.
2. Make small balls from the meat mixture.
3. Place the cooking pot in the unit then place the crisper basket in the pot.
4. Select air crisp mode set the temperature to 400 F and set the time to 12 minutes. Press start to begin preheating.
5. Once the unit is preheated then place meatballs in the crisper basket. Close with a lid and cook for 12 minutes.
6. Serve and enjoy.

Nutritional Value (Amount per Serving):

- Calories 385
- Fat 13.2 g
- Carbohydrates 7.6 g
- Sugar 1.2 g
- Protein 55.5 g
- Cholesterol 196 mg

Mini Meatloaf

Preparation Time: 10 minutes
Cooking Time: 12 minutes
Serve: 4

Ingredients:

- 1 egg
- 1 lb ground beef
- 1/4 cup BBQ sauce
- 1/2 tsp yellow mustard
- 1 tbsp Worcestershire sauce
- 1/2 tsp garlic powder
- 1/2 tsp onion powder
- 1/4 cup breadcrumbs
- 3/4 cup cheddar cheese, shredded
- 2 bacon slices, cooked & chopped
- 3 oz chili sauce
- 1/2 tsp salt

Directions:

1. Add all ingredients except BBQ sauce into the mixing bowl and mix until well combined.
2. Make four mini loaves from the meat mixture.
3. Place the cooking pot in the unit then place the crisper basket in the pot.
4. Select air crisp mode set the temperature to 400 F and set the time to 12 minutes. Press start to begin preheating.
5. Once the unit is preheated then place loaves in the crisper basket and brush top of loaves with BBQ sauce. Close with a lid and cook for 12 minutes.
6. Serve and enjoy.

Nutritional Value (Amount per Serving):

- Calories 422
- Fat 19.7 g
- Carbohydrates 12.7 g
- Sugar 5.9 g
- Protein 45.7 g
- Cholesterol 175 mg

Tasty Steak Bites

Preparation Time: 10 minutes
Cooking Time: 10 minutes
Serve: 2

Ingredients:

- 2 steaks, trimmed & cubed
- 1/2 tbsp olive oil
- 1/4 tbsp paprika
- 1/4 tbsp chili powder
- 1/2 tbsp garlic powder
- 1/4 cup brown sugar
- 1/2 tbsp salt

Directions:

1. In a mixing bowl, add steak cubes and oil and mix well.
2. In a small bowl, mix together paprika, chili powder, garlic powder, sugar, and salt and sprinkle over steak cubes and toss to coat.
3. Place the cooking pot in the unit then place the crisper basket in the pot.
4. Select air crisp mode set the temperature to 400 F and set the time to 10 minutes. Press start to begin preheating.
5. Once the unit is preheated then add steak cubes in the crisper basket. Close with a lid and cook for 10 minutes.
6. Stir steak cubes halfway through.
7. Serve and enjoy.

Nutritional Value (Amount per Serving):

- Calories 631
- Fat 16.8 g
- Carbohydrates 20.3 g
- Sugar 18.3 g
- Protein 94.9 g
- Cholesterol 235 mg

Meatballs

Preparation Time: 10 minutes
Cooking Time: 10 minutes
Serve: 4

Ingredients:

- 2 eggs
- 1 tsp sesame oil
- 1 tsp ginger, minced
- 1 tsp garlic, minced
- 1/2 cup breadcrumbs
- 1/3 tsp red chili pepper flakes
- 1 tbsp scallions, diced
- 1 tsp soy sauce
- 2 lbs ground pork
- Pepper
- Salt

Directions:

1. Add all ingredients into the large bowl and mix until well combined.
2. Make small balls from the meat mixture.
3. Place the cooking pot in the unit then place the crisper basket in the pot.
4. Select air crisp mode set the temperature to 400 F and set the time to 10 minutes. Press start to begin preheating.
5. Once the unit is preheated then place meatballs in the crisper basket. Close with a lid and cook for 10 minutes.
6. Serve and enjoy.

Nutritional Value (Amount per Serving):

- Calories 423
- Fat 12 g
- Carbohydrates 10.7 g
- Sugar 1.1 g
- Protein 64.1 g
- Cholesterol 247 mg

Mustard Meatballs

Preparation Time: 10 minutes
Cooking Time: 10 minutes
Serve: 4

Ingredients:

- 1 1/4 lbs ground pork
- 1 tsp ginger garlic paste
- 2 tsp honey
- 1 small onion, chopped
- 1 tsp pork seasoning
- Pepper
- Salt

Directions:

1. Add all ingredients into the mixing bowl and mix until well combined.
2. Make small balls from the meat mixture.
3. Place the cooking pot in the unit then place the crisper basket in the pot.
4. Select air crisp mode set the temperature to 360 F and set the time to 10 minutes. Press start to begin preheating.
5. Once the unit is preheated then place meatballs in the crisper basket. Close with a lid and cook for 10 minutes.
6. Serve and enjoy.

Nutritional Value (Amount per Serving):

- Calories 227
- Fat 5.3 g
- Carbohydrates 5.3 g
- Sugar 3.6 g
- Protein 37.6 g
- Cholesterol 103 mg

Spicy Pork Patties

Preparation Time: 10 minutes
Cooking Time: 10 minutes
Serve: 2

Ingredients:

- 1 egg, lightly beaten
- 1/2 lb ground pork
- 1 tbsp Cajun seasoning
- 1/2 cup breadcrumbs
- Pepper
- Salt

Directions:

1. Add all ingredients into the large bowl and mix until well combined.
2. Make two equal shapes of patties from the meat mixture.
3. Place the cooking pot in the unit then place the crisper basket in the pot.
4. Select air crisp mode set the temperature to 360 F and set the time to 10 minutes. Press start to begin preheating.
5. Once the unit is preheated then place patties in the crisper basket. Close with a lid and cook for 10 minutes.
6. Serve and enjoy.

Nutritional Value (Amount per Serving):

- Calories 300
- Fat 7.6 g
- Carbohydrates 19.6 g
- Sugar 1.8 g
- Protein 36.1 g
- Cholesterol 165 mg

Crispy Pork Chops

Preparation Time: 10 minutes
Cooking Time: 12 minutes
Serve: 3

Ingredients:

- 1 egg, lightly beaten
- 3 pork chops, boneless
- 1/2 cup breadcrumbs
- 1/4 tsp paprika
- 1/2 tsp garlic powder
- Pepper
- Salt

Directions:

1. Season pork chops with paprika, garlic powder, pepper, and salt.
2. Place breadcrumbs in a shallow bowl. In a separate shallow bowl, add beaten egg.
3. Dip pork chop in egg and coat with breadcrumb.
4. Place the cooking pot in the unit then place the crisper basket in the pot.
5. Select air crisp mode set the temperature to 380 F and set the time to 12 minutes. Press start to begin preheating.
6. Once the unit is preheated then place coated pork chops in the crisper basket. Close with a lid and cook for 12 minutes. Turn pork chops halfway through.
7. Serve and enjoy.

Nutritional Value (Amount per Serving):

- Calories 350
- Fat 22.3 g
- Carbohydrates 13.5 g
- Sugar 1.4 g
- Protein 22.3 g
- Cholesterol 123 mg

Herb Pork Chops

Preparation Time: 10 minutes
Cooking Time: 15 minutes
Serve: 4

Ingredients:

- 4 pork chops
- 1 tsp rosemary
- 2 tsp oregano
- 2 tsp thyme
- 1 tsp garlic powder
- 1 tsp paprika
- Pepper
- Salt

Directions:

1. Spray pork chops with cooking spray.
2. Mix together garlic powder, paprika, rosemary, oregano, thyme, pepper, and salt and rub over pork chops.
3. Place the cooking pot in the unit then place the crisper basket in the pot.
4. Select air crisp mode set the temperature to 360 F and set the time to 15 minutes. Press start to begin preheating.
5. Once the unit is preheated then place pork chops in the crisper basket. Close with a lid and cook for 15 minutes. Turn pork chops halfway through.
6. Serve and enjoy.

Nutritional Value (Amount per Serving):

- Calories 265
- Fat 20.1 g
- Carbohydrates 1.8 g
- Sugar 0.3 g
- Protein 18.3 g
- Cholesterol 69 mg

Flavorful Honey Pork Chops

Preparation Time: 10 minutes
Cooking Time: 12 minutes
Serve: 4

Ingredients:

- 1 lb pork chops, boneless
- 2 tsp honey
- 1 tbsp yellow mustard
- 1 tsp steak seasoning

Directions:

1. In a small bowl, mix together honey, mustard, and steak seasoning.
2. Brush pork chops with honey mixture.
3. Place the cooking pot in the unit then place the crisper basket in the pot.
4. Select air crisp mode set the temperature to 350 F and set the time to 12 minutes. Press start to begin preheating.
5. Once the unit is preheated then place pork chops in the crisper basket. Close with a lid and cook for 12 minutes. Turn pork chops halfway through.
6. Serve and enjoy.

Nutritional Value (Amount per Serving):

- Calories 376
- Fat 28.3 g
- Carbohydrates 3.1 g
- Sugar 2.9 g
- Protein 25.7 g
- Cholesterol 98 mg

Juicy Pork Chops

Preparation Time: 10 minutes
Cooking Time: 14 minutes
Serve: 2

Ingredients:

- 2 pork chops
- 1 tsp olive oil
- 1 tsp garlic powder
- 1 tsp smoked paprika
- Pepper
- Salt

Directions:

1. Brush pork chops with oil and season with garlic powder, paprika, pepper, and salt.
2. Place the cooking pot in the unit then place the crisper basket in the pot.
3. Select air crisp mode set the temperature to 360 F and set the time to 14 minutes. Press start to begin preheating.
4. Once the unit is preheated then place pork chops in the crisper basket. Close with a lid and cook for 14 minutes. Turn pork chops halfway through.
5. Serve and enjoy.

Nutritional Value (Amount per Serving):

- Calories 284
- Fat 22.4 g
- Carbohydrates 1.6 g
- Sugar 0.5 g
- Protein 18.4 g
- Cholesterol 69 mg

Easy Pork Bites

Preparation Time: 10 minutes
Cooking Time: 15 minutes
Serve: 4

Ingredients:

- 1 lb pork belly, cut into 3/4-inch cubes
- 1 tsp soy sauce
- 1/2 tsp garlic powder
- 1/2 tsp onion powder
- Pepper
- Salt

Directions:

1. In a mixing bowl, toss pork cubes with onion powder, garlic powder, soy sauce, pepper, and salt.
2. Place the cooking pot in the unit then place the crisper basket in the pot.
3. Select air crisp mode set the temperature to 400 F and set the time to 15 minutes. Press start to begin preheating.
4. Once the unit is preheated then place pork cubes in the crisper basket. Close with a lid and cook for 15 minutes. Stir pork cubes halfway through.
5. Serve and enjoy.

Nutritional Value (Amount per Serving):

- Calories 526
- Fat 30.5 g
- Carbohydrates 0.6 g
- Sugar 0.2 g
- Protein 52.5 g
- Cholesterol 131 mg

Delicious Pork Chops

Preparation Time: 10 minutes
Cooking Time: 16 minutes
Serve: 2

Ingredients:

- 2 pork chops
- 1 tbsp olive oil
- 1 tbsp mesquite seasoning
- 2 tbsp honey
- Pepper
- Salt

Directions:

1. Mix together olive oil, honey, mesquite seasoning, pepper, and salt and rub all over pork chops.
2. Place pork chops into the mixing bowl. Cover bowl and place in the refrigerator for 30 minutes.
3. Place the cooking pot in the unit then place the crisper basket in the pot.
4. Select air crisp mode set the temperature to 380 F and set the time to 16 minutes. Press start to begin preheating.
5. Once the unit is preheated then place marinated pork chops in the crisper basket. Close with a lid and cook for 15 minutes. Turn pork chops halfway through.
6. Serve and enjoy.

Nutritional Value (Amount per Serving):

- Calories 387
- Fat 27 g
- Carbohydrates 18.5 g
- Sugar 17.3 g
- Protein 18.3 g
- Cholesterol 69 mg

Simple & Tasty Pork Chops

Preparation Time: 10 minutes
Cooking Time: 35 minutes
Serve: 2

Ingredients:

- 2 pork chops
- 2 tbsp brown sugar
- 2 tbsp tomato sauce
- Pepper
- Salt

Directions:

1. Season pork chops with pepper and salt.
2. Place pork chops in a baking dish.
3. Mix together ketchup and brown sugar and pour over pork chops.
4. Place the cooking pot in the unit.
5. Select bake mode set the temperature to 375 F and set the time to 35 minutes. Press start to begin preheating.
6. Once the unit is preheated then place the baking dish in the cooking pot. Close with a lid and cook for 35 minutes.
7. Serve and enjoy.

Nutritional Value (Amount per Serving):

- Calories 294
- Fat 19.9 g
- Carbohydrates 9.7 g
- Sugar 9.4 g
- Protein 18.2 g
- Cholesterol 69 mg

Meatballs

Preparation Time: 10 minutes
Cooking Time: 15 minutes
Serve: 4

Ingredients:

- 1 lb ground pork
- 1 tsp paprika
- 1 tsp garlic powder
- 1 tsp onion powder
- 1/2 tsp ground cumin
- 1/2 tsp coriander
- 1/2 tsp dried thyme
- Pepper
- Salt

Directions:

1. Add all ingredients into the large bowl and mix until well combined.
2. Make small balls from the meat mixture.
3. Place the cooking pot in the unit.
4. Select bake mode set the temperature to 400 F and set the time to 15 minutes. Press start to begin preheating.
5. Once the unit is preheated then place meatballs in the cooking pot. Close with a lid and cook for 15 minutes.
6. Serve and enjoy.

Nutritional Value (Amount per Serving):

- Calories 170
- Fat 4.1 g
- Carbohydrates 1.5 g
- Sugar 0.4 g
- Protein 30 g
- Cholesterol 83 mg

Chapter 5: Fish & Seafood

Grilled Salmon Patties

Preparation Time: 10 minutes
Cooking Time: 8 minutes
Serve: 6

Ingredients:

- 2 eggs
- 1 lb salmon fillet, remove skin
- 1/4 cup fresh parsley, chopped
- 1 cup breadcrumbs
- 1 tsp mustard
- 1 tbsp fresh lime juice
- 1/4 cup mayonnaise
- 1/2 tsp pepper
- 1/2 tsp salt

Directions:

1. Add all ingredients into the bowl and mix until well combined.
2. Make six equal shapes of patties from the mixture.
3. Place the cooking pot in the unit then place the grill plate in the pot.
4. Select grill mode set the temperature to medium and set the time to 8 minutes. Press start to begin preheating.
5. Once the unit is preheated then place patties on the grill plate. Close with a lid and cook for 8 minutes. Flip patties halfway through.
6. Serve and enjoy.

Nutritional Value (Amount per Serving):

- Calories 234
- Fat 10.5 g
- Carbohydrates 16.5 g
- Sugar 2 g
- Protein 19.3 g
- Cholesterol 90 mg

Lemon Garlic Salmon

Preparation Time: 10 minutes
Cooking Time: 8 minutes
Serve: 4

Ingredients:

- 1 1/2 lbs salmon fillets
- 1/4 cup olive oil
- 1 lemon juice
- 1/2 tsp pepper
- 1 tsp dried oregano
- 2 garlic cloves, minced
- 1 tsp sea salt

Directions:

1. In a large bowl, mix oregano, garlic, oil, lemon juice, pepper, and salt.
2. Add salmon fillets and coat well. Cover and place in the refrigerator for 15 minutes.
3. Place the cooking pot in the unit then place the grill plate in the pot.
4. Select grill mode set the temperature to medium and set the time to 8 minutes. Press start to begin preheating.
5. Once the unit is preheated then place fish fillets on the grill plate. Close with a lid and cook for 8 minutes. Flip fish fillets halfway through.
6. Serve and enjoy.

Nutritional Value (Amount per Serving):

- Calories 340
- Fat 23.3 g
- Carbohydrates 1.2 g
- Sugar 0.3 g
- Protein 33.3 g
- Cholesterol 75 mg

Flavorful Mahi Mahi

Preparation Time: 10 minutes
Cooking Time: 10 minutes
Serve: 2

Ingredients:

- 2 mahi-mahi fillets
- 1/2 tsp onion powder
- 1/2 tsp garlic powder
- 1 tsp paprika
- 3 tbsp olive oil
- 2 tbsp fresh lime juice
- 1 tsp cumin
- 1 tsp dried oregano
- 1/8 tsp cayenne
- Pepper
- Salt

Directions:

1. In a small bowl, mix cumin, oregano, cayenne, garlic powder, paprika, pepper, and salt.
2. Brush fish fillets with oil and season with spice mixture.
3. Place the cooking pot in the unit then place the grill plate in the pot.
4. Select grill mode set the temperature to medium and set the time to 8 minutes. Press start to begin preheating.
5. Once the unit is preheated then place fish fillets on the grill plate. Close with a lid and cook for 10 minutes. Flip fish fillets halfway through.
6. Drizzle fish fillets with lime juice and serve.

Nutritional Value (Amount per Serving):

- Calories 295
- Fat 21.5 g
- Carbohydrates 6.3 g
- Sugar 1.3 g
- Protein 21.8 g
- Cholesterol 40 mg

Blackened Cod

Preparation Time: 10 minutes
Cooking Time: 8 minutes
Serve: 4

Ingredients:

- 4 cod fillets
- 1 tbsp olive oil
- 2 tbsp blackened seasoning
- 1/2 tsp kosher salt

Directions:

1. Brush cod fillets with oil and season with blackened seasoning and salt.
2. Place the cooking pot in the unit then place the grill plate in the pot.
3. Select grill mode set the temperature to medium and set the time to 8 minutes. Press start to begin preheating.
4. Once the unit is preheated then place fish fillets on the grill plate. Close with a lid and cook for 8 minutes. Flip fish fillets halfway through.
5. Serve and enjoy.

Nutritional Value (Amount per Serving):

- Calories 120
- Fat 4.5 g
- Carbohydrates 0 g
- Sugar 0 g
- Protein 20 g
- Cholesterol 55 mg

Spicy Shrimp

Preparation Time: 10 minutes
Cooking Time: 6 minutes
Serve: 4

Ingredients:

- 1 lb shrimp, peeled and deveined
- 1 tsp garlic powder
- 1 tsp onion powder
- 2 tbsp olive oil
- 2 tsp paprika
- 1/4 tsp cayenne
- 1 tsp dried oregano
- Pepper
- Salt

Directions:

1. In a large bowl, toss shrimp with remaining ingredients.
2. Place the cooking pot in the unit then place the crisper basket in the pot.
3. Select air crisp mode set the temperature to 400 F and set the time to 6 minutes. Press start to begin preheating.
4. Once the unit is preheated then place shrimp in the crisper basket. Close with a lid and cook for 6 minutes.
5. Serve and enjoy.

Nutritional Value (Amount per Serving):

- Calories 204
- Fat 9.1 g
- Carbohydrates 3.6 g
- Sugar 0.5 g
- Protein 26.2 g
- Cholesterol 239 mg

Dijon Salmon Fillets

Preparation Time: 10 minutes
Cooking Time: 15 minutes
Serve: 4

Ingredients:

- 1 lb salmon fillets
- 1/4 cup brown sugar
- 2 tbsp Dijon mustard
- Pepper
- Salt

Directions:

1. Season salmon fillets with pepper and salt.
2. In a small bowl, mix together Dijon mustard and brown sugar.
3. Brush salmon fillets with Dijon mustard mixture.
4. Place the cooking pot in the unit then place the crisper basket in the pot.
5. Select air crisp mode set the temperature to 350 F and set the time to 15 minutes. Press start to begin preheating.
6. Once the unit is preheated then place salmon fillets in the crisper basket. Close with a lid and cook for 15 minutes.
7. Serve and enjoy.

Nutritional Value (Amount per Serving):

- Calories 190
- Fat 7.3 g
- Carbohydrates 9.3 g
- Sugar 8.9 g
- Protein 22.4 g
- Cholesterol 50 mg

Cajun Fish Fillets

Preparation Time: 10 minutes
Cooking Time: 15 minutes
Serve: 2

Ingredients:

- 2 white fish fillets
- 2 tsp Cajun seasoning
- 1/2 cup cornmeal

Directions:

1. In a shallow dish, mix together cornmeal and Cajun seasoning.
2. Spray fish fillets with cooking spray and coat with cornmeal.
3. Place the cooking pot in the unit then place the crisper basket in the pot.
4. Select air crisp mode set the temperature to 390 F and set the time to 15 minutes. Press start to begin preheating.
5. Once the unit is preheated then place coated fish fillets in the crisper basket. Close with a lid and cook for 15 minutes.
6. Serve and enjoy.

Nutritional Value (Amount per Serving):

- Calories 375
- Fat 12.7 g
- Carbohydrates 23.5 g
- Sugar 0.2 g
- Protein 40.2 g
- Cholesterol 119 mg

Sweet & Spicy Salmon

Preparation Time: 10 minutes
Cooking Time: 12 minutes
Serve: 2

Ingredients:

- 2 salmon fillets
- 1/2 tsp chili powder
- 1 1/2 tsp coriander
- 1/4 cup honey
- 1 tbsp chili flakes, crushed
- 1/2 tsp turmeric
- Pepper
- Salt

Directions:

1. In a small bowl, mix honey, chili powder, chili flakes, coriander, turmeric, pepper, and salt.
2. Brush salmon fillets with honey mixture.
3. Place the cooking pot in the unit then place the crisper basket in the pot.
4. Select air crisp mode set the temperature to 400 F and set the time to 12 minutes. Press start to begin preheating.
5. Once the unit is preheated then place fish fillets in the crisper basket. Close with a lid and cook for 12 minutes.
6. Serve and enjoy.

Nutritional Value (Amount per Serving):

- Calories 369
- Fat 11.2 g
- Carbohydrates 35.8 g
- Sugar 35 g
- Protein 34.8 g
- Cholesterol 78 mg

Tasty Crab Cakes

Preparation Time: 10 minutes
Cooking Time: 10 minutes
Serve: 4

Ingredients:

- 8 oz crab meat
- 2 tbsp mayonnaise
- 2 green onion, chopped
- 1/4 cup bell pepper, chopped
- 1 tsp old bay seasoning
- 1 tbsp Dijon mustard
- 2 tbsp breadcrumbs
- Pepper
- Salt

Directions:

1. Add all ingredients into the bowl and mix until well combined.
2. Make four equal shapes of patties from the mixture.
3. Place the cooking pot in the unit then place the crisper basket in the pot.
4. Select air crisp mode set the temperature to 370 F and set the time to 10 minutes. Press start to begin preheating.
5. Once the unit is preheated then place patties in the crisper basket. Close with a lid and cook for 10 minutes.
6. Serve and enjoy.

Nutritional Value (Amount per Serving):

- Calories 100
- Fat 3.8 g
- Carbohydrates 6.5 g
- Sugar 1.3 g
- Protein 8 g
- Cholesterol 32 mg

Lemon Pepper Shrimp

Preparation Time: 10 minutes
Cooking Time: 8 minutes
Serve: 2

Ingredients:

- 12 oz shrimp, peeled and deveined
- 1 tsp lemon pepper
- 1 lemon juice
- 1/2 tbsp olive oil
- Salt

Directions:

1. In a large bowl, mix together lemon juice, lemon pepper, and salt. Add shrimp and toss until well coated.
2. Place the cooking pot in the unit then place the crisper basket in the pot.
3. Select air crisp mode set the temperature to 400 F and set the time to 8 minutes. Press start to begin preheating.
4. Once the unit is preheated then place shrimp in the crisper basket. Close with a lid and cook for 8 minutes.
5. Serve and enjoy.

Nutritional Value (Amount per Serving):

- Calories 240
- Fat 6.6 g
- Carbohydrates 3.8 g
- Sugar 0.5 g
- Protein 39 g
- Cholesterol 358 mg

Spicy Scallops

Preparation Time: 10 minutes
Cooking Time: 6 minutes
Serve: 2

Ingredients:

- 4 scallops, rinsed and pat dry
- 1/2 tsp Cajun seasoning
- Pepper
- Salt

Directions:

1. Spray scallops with cooking spray and season with Cajun seasoning, pepper, and salt.
2. Place the cooking pot in the unit then place the crisper basket in the pot.
3. Select air crisp mode set the temperature to 400 F and set the time to 6 minutes. Press start to begin preheating.
4. Once the unit is preheated then place scallops in the crisper basket. Close with a lid and cook for 6 minutes. Turn scallops halfway through.
5. Serve and enjoy.

Nutritional Value (Amount per Serving):

- Calories 53
- Fat 0.5 g
- Carbohydrates 1.5 g
- Sugar 0 g
- Protein 10.1 g
- Cholesterol 20 mg

Baked Halibut

Preparation Time: 10 minutes
Cooking Time: 12 minutes
Serve: 4

Ingredients:

- 1 lb halibut fillets
- 1/4 tsp pepper
- 1/4 cup olive oil
- 1 lime juice
- 1/4 tsp garlic powder
- 1/4 tsp paprika
- 1/2 tsp salt

Directions:

1. In a small bowl, mix together oil, lime juice, pepper, paprika, garlic powder, and salt.
2. Brush oil mixture over fish fillets.
3. Place the cooking pot in the unit.
4. Select bake mode set the temperature to 400 F and set the time to 12 minutes. Press start to begin preheating.
5. Once the unit is preheated then place fish fillets in the cooking pot. Close with a lid and cook for 12 minutes.
6. Serve and enjoy.

Nutritional Value (Amount per Serving):

- Calories 238
- Fat 15.3 g
- Carbohydrates 1.2 g
- Sugar 0.2 g
- Protein 24 g
- Cholesterol 36 mg

Bagel Fish Fillets

Preparation Time: 10 minutes
Cooking Time: 10 minutes
Serve: 4

Ingredients:

- 4 white fish fillets
- 2 tbsp almond flour
- 1/4 cup bagel seasoning
- 1 tbsp mayonnaise
- 1 tsp lemon pepper seasoning

Directions:

1. In a small bowl, mix together bagel seasoning, almond flour, and lemon pepper seasoning.
2. Brush mayonnaise over fish fillets. Sprinkle seasoning mixture over fish fillets.
3. Place the cooking pot in the unit.
4. Select bake mode set the temperature to 400 F and set the time to 10 minutes. Press start to begin preheating.
5. Once the unit is preheated then place fish fillets in the cooking pot. Close with a lid and cook for 10 minutes.
6. Serve and enjoy.

Nutritional Value (Amount per Serving):

- Calories 375
- Fat 19.9 g
- Carbohydrates 7.2 g
- Sugar 1 g
- Protein 41.3 g
- Cholesterol 120 mg

Delicious Tuna Steaks

Preparation Time: 10 minutes
Cooking Time: 4 minutes
Serve: 2

Ingredients:

- 12 tuna steaks, skinless and boneless
- 1 tsp ginger, grated
- 4 tbsp soy sauce
- 1/2 tsp vinegar
- 1 tsp sesame oil

Directions:

1. Add tuna steaks and remaining ingredients in the zip-lock bag. Seal bag and place in the refrigerator for 30 minutes.
2. Place the cooking pot in the unit then place the crisper basket in the pot.
3. Select air crisp mode set the temperature to 380 F and set the time to 4 minutes. Press start to begin preheating.
4. Once the unit is preheated then place tuna steaks in the crisper basket. Close with a lid and cook for 4 minutes.
5. Serve and enjoy.

Nutritional Value (Amount per Serving):

- Calories 979
- Fat 34.4 g
- Carbohydrates 3.1 g
- Sugar 0.6 g
- Protein 154.6 g
- Cholesterol 250 mg

Easy Lemon Pepper Fish Fillets

Preparation Time: 10 minutes
Cooking Time: 15 minutes
Serve: 4

Ingredients:

- 4 white fish fillets
- 4 tbsp lemon pepper seasoning

Directions:

1. Spray fish fillets with cooking spray.
2. Sprinkle lemon pepper seasoning over fish fillets.
3. Place the cooking pot in the unit.
4. Select bake mode set the temperature to 350 F and set the time to 15 minutes. Press start to begin preheating.
5. Once the unit is preheated then place fish fillets in the cooking pot. Close with a lid and cook for 15 minutes.
6. Serve and enjoy.

Nutritional Value (Amount per Serving):

- Calories 281
- Fat 11.8 g
- Carbohydrates 4.2 g
- Sugar 0 g
- Protein 38.4 g
- Cholesterol 119 mg

Chapter 6: Vegetable & Side Dishes

Healthy Spinach Casserole

Preparation Time: 10 minutes
Cooking Time: 20 minutes
Serve: 6

Ingredients:

- 2 lbs baby spinach
- 1 cup parmesan cheese, grated
- 1 tbsp Italian seasoning
- 1 tbsp garlic, minced
- 3 tbsp olive oil
- 5 tbsp butter
- 3/4 tsp salt

Directions:

1. Add 5 cups of water to the stockpot and bring to boil. Add spinach and cook until wilted. Drain well.
2. Melt butter in a pan over medium-low heat.
3. Add garlic, Italian seasoning, and salt and cook for 1-2 minutes.
4. Spread spinach in a greased baking dish then drizzles with butter mixture.
5. Sprinkle cheese over spinach.
6. Place the cooking pot in the unit.
7. Select bake mode set the temperature to 400 F and set the time to 15 minutes. Press start to begin preheating.
8. Once the unit is preheated then place the baking dish in the cooking pot. Close with a lid and cook for 15 minutes.
9. Serve and enjoy.

Nutritional Value (Amount per Serving):

- Calories 237
- Fat 21.1 g
- Carbohydrates 6.8 g
- Sugar 0.9 g
- Protein 9.3 g
- Cholesterol 38 mg

Tasty Cauliflower Steaks

Preparation Time: 10 minutes
Cooking Time: 10 minutes
Serve: 4

Ingredients:

- 1 medium cauliflower head, cut into 1/2-inch thick slices
- 1/2 cup parmesan cheese, grated
- 1/2 tsp dried thyme
- 2 tbsp soy sauce
- 1 tbsp garlic, minced
- 1/4 cup olive oil
- 1/2 tsp onion powder
- 1/2 tsp chili powder
- 1/2 tsp lemon pepper seasoning
- Pepper
- Salt

Directions:

1. In a small bowl, mix onion powder, chili powder, lemon pepper seasoning, thyme, soy sauce, garlic, olive oil, pepper, and salt.
2. Brush cauliflower slices with spice and oil mixture.
3. Place the cooking pot in the unit then place the grill plate in the pot.
4. Select grill mode set the temperature to medium and set the time to 8 minutes. Press start to begin preheating.
5. Once the unit is preheated then place cauliflower slices on the grill plate. Close with a lid and cook for 10 minutes. Turn cauliflower slices halfway through.
6. Sprinkle with cheese and serve.

Nutritional Value (Amount per Serving):

- Calories 191
- Fat 15.2 g
- Carbohydrates 10 g
- Sugar 3.7 g
- Protein 7.2 g
- Cholesterol 8 mg

Flavorful Sweet Potatoes

Preparation Time: 10 minutes
Cooking Time: 6 minutes
Serve: 4

Ingredients:

- 2 large sweet potatoes, sliced thinly
- 1/2 tsp paprika
- 1 tsp chili powder
- 1 1/2 tbsp olive oil
- 1/4 tsp chili powder
- 1 tsp garlic powder
- 1/2 tsp cumin

Directions:

1. Add sweet potato slices and remaining ingredients into the mixing bowl and toss well.
2. Place the cooking pot in the unit then place the grill plate in the pot.
3. Select grill mode set the temperature to medium and set the time to 8 minutes. Press start to begin preheating.
4. Once the unit is preheated then place sweet potato slices on the grill plate. Close with a lid and cook for 3 minutes. Flip sweet potato slices halfway through.
5. Serve and enjoy.

Nutritional Value (Amount per Serving):

- Calories 140
- Fat 5.6 g
- Carbohydrates 22 g
- Sugar 0.6 g
- Protein 1.4 g
- Cholesterol 0 mg

Zucchini Spinach Casserole

Preparation Time: 10 minutes
Cooking Time: 45 minutes
Serve: 6

Ingredients:

- 2 egg whites
- 1/4 cup parmesan cheese, grated
- 1/4 cup feta cheese, crumbled
- 2 small yellow squash, diced
- 2 small zucchini, diced
- 3 cups baby spinach
- 1 tsp dried basil
- 1/2 tsp pepper
- 2 tsp garlic powder
- 1/4 cup breadcrumbs
- 2 tbsp olive oil
- 1/2 tsp kosher salt

Directions:

1. Heat oil in a pan over medium heat.
2. Add squash, zucchini, and spinach and cook for 5 minutes or until spinach is wilted. Transfer squash mixture into the mixing bowl.
3. Add remaining ingredients to the mixing bowl and mix well.
4. Pour mixture into the greased baking dish.
5. Place the cooking pot in the unit.
6. Select bake mode set the temperature to 400 F and set the time to 40 minutes. Press start to begin preheating.
7. Once the unit is preheated then place the baking dish in the cooking pot. Close with a lid and cook.
8. Serve and enjoy.

Nutritional Value (Amount per Serving):

- Calories 112
- Fat 7.3 g
- Carbohydrates 7.7 g
- Sugar 2.3 g
- Protein 5.5 g
- Cholesterol 8 mg

Delicious Zucchini Sticks

Preparation Time: 10 minutes
Cooking Time: 15 minutes
Serve: 8

Ingredients:

- 4 medium zucchini, cut in half lengthwise & scoop out the middle
- 1 tbsp garlic, minced
- 1/2 cup olives, chopped
- 1/2 cup tomatoes, chopped
- 1 cup red bell pepper, chopped
- 1/4 cup parsley, chopped
- 1/4 cup feta cheese, crumbled
- 1 tbsp dried oregano
- 1/4 tsp pepper

Directions:

1. In a bowl, mix bell pepper, pepper, oregano, garlic, olives, and tomato.
2. Stuff each zucchini with bell pepper mixture.
3. Place the cooking pot in the unit.
4. Select bake mode set the temperature to 350 F and set the time to 15 minutes. Press start to begin preheating.
5. Once the unit is preheated then place stuffed zucchini in the cooking pot. Close with a lid and cook.
6. Garnish with parsley and serve.

Nutritional Value (Amount per Serving):

- Calories 49
- Fat 2.2 g
- Carbohydrates 6.5 g
- Sugar 3 g
- Protein 2.4 g
- Cholesterol 4 mg

Stuffed Peppers

Preparation Time: 10 minutes
Cooking Time: 25 minutes
Serve: 6

Ingredients:

- 3 bell peppers, cut in half & remove seeds
- 1/3 cup chickpeas, rinsed
- 1/2 tsp oregano
- 2 garlic cloves, minced
- 1 1/2 cups cooked quinoa
- 1/4 cup feta cheese, crumbled
- 1/2 cup grape tomatoes, sliced
- 1/2 tsp salt

Directions:

1. In a bowl, mix cooked quinoa, tomatoes, chickpeas, oregano, garlic, and salt.
2. Stuff quinoa mixture into the bell pepper halves.
3. Place the cooking pot in the unit.
4. Select bake mode set the temperature to 400 F and set the time to 25 minutes. Press start to begin preheating.
5. Once the unit is preheated then place stuffed peppers in the cooking pot. Close with a lid and cook.
6. Serve and enjoy.

Nutritional Value (Amount per Serving):

- Calories 237
- Fat 4.8 g
- Carbohydrates 39.8 g
- Sugar 4.9 g
- Protein 9.8 g
- Cholesterol 6 mg

Flavorful Baby Potatoes

Preparation Time: 10 minutes
Cooking Time: 20 minutes
Serve: 4

Ingredients:

- 1 lb baby potatoes, cut into quarters
- 1/2 tsp granulated garlic
- 1 tbsp olive oil
- 1/2 tsp dried parsley
- 1/4 tsp salt

Directions:

1. In a mixing bowl, toss baby potatoes with oil, garlic, parsley, and salt.
2. Place the cooking pot in the unit then place the crisper basket in the pot.
3. Select air crisp mode set the temperature to 350 F and set the time to 20 minutes. Press start to begin preheating.
4. Once the unit is preheated then place potatoes in the crisper basket. Close with a lid and cook.
5. Serve and enjoy.

Nutritional Value (Amount per Serving):

- Calories 97
- Fat 3.6 g
- Carbohydrates 14.4 g
- Sugar 0.1 g
- Protein 3 g
- Cholesterol 0 mg

Tasty Hasselback Potatoes

Preparation Time: 10 minutes
Cooking Time: 30 minutes
Serve: 4

Ingredients:

- 4 potatoes, peel & cut potato across the potato to make 1/8-inch slices
- 1/4 cup parmesan cheese, shredded
- 1 tbsp olive oil

Directions:

1. Brush potatoes with oil.
2. Place the cooking pot in the unit then place the crisper basket in the pot.
3. Select air crisp mode set the temperature to 350 F and set the time to 30 minutes. Press start to begin preheating.
4. Once the unit is preheated then place potatoes in the crisper basket. Close with a lid and cook.
5. Sprinkle potatoes with parmesan cheese and serve.

Nutritional Value (Amount per Serving):

- Calories 195
- Fat 4.9 g
- Carbohydrates 33.7 g
- Sugar 2.5 g
- Protein 5.4 g
- Cholesterol 4 mg

Spicy Brussels Sprouts

Preparation Time: 10 minutes
Cooking Time: 15 minutes
Serve: 4

Ingredients:

- 1 lb Brussels sprouts, cut in half
- 1 1/2 tbsp olive oil
- 2 tbsp honey
- 1 tbsp gochujang
- 1/2 tsp salt

Directions:

1. In a large bowl, mix together olive oil, honey, gochujang, and salt.
2. Add Brussels sprouts into the bowl and toss until well coated.
3. Place the cooking pot in the unit then place the crisper basket in the pot.
4. Select air crisp mode set the temperature to 360 F and set the time to 15 minutes. Press start to begin preheating.
5. Once the unit is preheated then place brussels sprouts in the crisper basket. Close with a lid and cook.
6. Serve and enjoy.

Nutritional Value (Amount per Serving):

- Calories 137
- Fat 5.6 g
- Carbohydrates 21.5 g
- Sugar 12.6 g
- Protein 4.2 g
- Cholesterol 0 mg

Mexican Potatoes

Preparation Time: 10 minutes
Cooking Time: 15 minutes
Serve: 4

Ingredients:

- 2 large sweet potatoes, peeled & cut into 1-inch pieces
- 1 tbsp chili powder
- 2 tbsp olive oil
- 2 tsp fresh lime juice
- 1 tsp cumin

Directions:

1. In a mixing bowl, add sweet potatoes, lime juice, cumin, chili powder, and olive oil and toss well.
2. Place the cooking pot in the unit then place the crisper basket in the pot.
3. Select air crisp mode set the temperature to 380 F and set the time to 15 minutes. Press start to begin preheating.
4. Once the unit is preheated then place potatoes in the crisper basket. Close with a lid and cook for 15 minutes. Stir sweet potatoes halfway through.
5. Serve and enjoy.

Nutritional Value (Amount per Serving):

- Calories 162
- Fat 7.6 g
- Carbohydrates 24 g
- Sugar 0.9 g
- Protein 1.6 g
- Cholesterol 0 mg

Zucchini Burger Patties

Preparation Time: 10 minutes
Cooking Time: 12 minutes
Serve: 4

Ingredients:

- 1 large zucchini, grated & squeeze out all liquid
- 1 tsp cumin
- 3 tbsp coriander
- 2 tbsp spring onion, sliced
- 7 oz can chickpeas, drained
- 1 tsp mixed spice
- 1 tsp chili powder
- Pepper
- Salt

Directions:

1. Add all ingredients into the mixing bowl and mix until well combined.
2. Make four equal shapes of patties from the mixture.
3. Place the cooking pot in the unit then place the crisper basket in the pot.
4. Select air crisp mode set the temperature to 400 F and set the time to 12 minutes. Press start to begin preheating.
5. Once the unit is preheated then place patties in the crisper basket. Close with a lid and cook for 12 minutes. Turn patties halfway through.
6. Serve and enjoy.

Nutritional Value (Amount per Serving):

- Calories 77
- Fat 1 g
- Carbohydrates 14.8 g
- Sugar 1.5 g
- Protein 3.7 g
- Cholesterol 0 mg

Healthy Asparagus

Preparation Time: 10 minutes
Cooking Time: 15 minutes
Serve: 4

Ingredients:

- 30 asparagus spears, cut the ends
- 1/2 tsp garlic powder
- 1 tbsp olive oil
- Pepper
- Salt

Directions:

1. Add asparagus into the large bowl. Drizzle with oil.
2. Sprinkle with garlic powder, pepper, and salt. Toss well.
3. Place the cooking pot in the unit then place the crisper basket in the pot.
4. Select air crisp mode set the temperature to 400 F and set the time to 15 minutes. Press start to begin preheating.
5. Once the unit is preheated then arrange asparagus spears in the crisper basket. Close with a lid and cook.
6. Serve and enjoy.

Nutritional Value (Amount per Serving):

- Calories 67
- Fat 3.7 g
- Carbohydrates 7.3 g
- Sugar 3.5 g
- Protein 4 g
- Cholesterol 0 mg

Easy Herb Mushrooms

Preparation Time: 10 minutes
Cooking Time: 14 minutes
Serve: 4

Ingredients:

- 1 lb mushrooms
- 1 tbsp basil, minced
- 1 tsp rosemary, chopped
- 1 garlic clove, minced
- 1/2 tbsp vinegar
- 1/2 tsp ground coriander
- Pepper
- Salt

Directions:

1. Add all ingredients into the large bowl and toss well.
2. Place the cooking pot in the unit then place the crisper basket in the pot.
3. Select air crisp mode set the temperature to 350 F and set the time to 14 minutes. Press start to begin preheating.
4. Once the unit is preheated then place mushrooms in the crisper basket. Close with a lid and cook for 14 minutes.
5. Serve and enjoy.

Nutritional Value (Amount per Serving):

- Calories 27
- Fat 0.4 g
- Carbohydrates 4.2 g
- Sugar 2 g
- Protein 3.6 g
- Cholesterol 0 mg

Baked Carrots

Preparation Time: 10 minutes
Cooking Time: 30 minutes
Serve: 4

Ingredients:

- 25 baby carrots
- 1 tsp cinnamon
- 6 tbsp butter, melted
- 1/4 cup brown sugar
- Pepper
- Salt

Directions:

1. Arrange baby carrots in the baking dish. Pour melted butter over baby carrots.
2. Sprinkle cinnamon, brown sugar, pepper, and salt over baby carrots.
3. Place the cooking pot in the unit.
4. Select bake mode set the temperature to 390 F and set the time to 30 minutes. Press start to begin preheating.
5. Once the unit is preheated then place the baking dish in the cooking pot. Close with a lid and cook.
6. Serve and enjoy.

Nutritional Value (Amount per Serving):

- Calories 211
- Fat 17.4 g
- Carbohydrates 14.5 g
- Sugar 11.8 g
- Protein 0.6 g
- Cholesterol 46 mg

Baked Zucchini Casserole

Preparation Time: 10 minutes
Cooking Time: 40 minutes
Serve: 8

Ingredients:

- 4 eggs, lightly beaten
- 4 cups zucchini, sliced
- 1 tbsp butter, melted
- 2 cups crushed crackers
- 1 1/2 cup milk
- 2 cups cheddar cheese, shredded

Directions:

1. Add sliced zucchini into the greased baking dish.
2. In a bowl, whisk together eggs, butter, milk, and 1 cup cheese and pour over sliced zucchini. Sprinkle with crushed crackers and remaining cheese.
3. Place the cooking pot in the unit.
4. Select bake mode set the temperature to 350 F and set the time to 40 minutes. Press start to begin preheating.
5. Once the unit is preheated then place the baking dish in the cooking pot. Close with a lid and cook.
6. Serve and enjoy.

Nutritional Value (Amount per Serving):

- Calories 220
- Fat 15.5 g
- Carbohydrates 8.4 g
- Sugar 4.1 g
- Protein 12.5 g
- Cholesterol 119 mg

Chapter 7: Snacks & Appetizers

Healthy & Delicious Roasted Peas

Preparation Time: 10 minutes
Cooking Time: 15 minutes
Serve: 2

Ingredients:

- 1 cup frozen peas, defrost & pat dry with a paper towel
- 1 tsp garlic powder
- 1/8 tsp chili powder
- 1 tsp olive oil
- Salt

Directions:

1. Add peas, garlic powder, chili powder, oil, and salt to the mixing bowl and mix well.
2. Place the cooking pot in the unit then place the crisper basket in the pot.
3. Select air crisp mode set the temperature to 350 F and set the time to 15 minutes. Press start to begin preheating.
4. Once the unit is preheated then place peas in the crisper basket. Close with a lid and cook for 15 minutes. Stir peas halfway through.
5. Serve and enjoy.

Nutritional Value (Amount per Serving):

- Calories 88
- Fat 2.6 g
- Carbohydrates 12.5 g
- Sugar 4.1 g
- Protein 4.4 g
- Cholesterol 0 mg

Tasty Roasted Chickpeas

Preparation Time: 10 minutes
Cooking Time: 20 minutes
Serve: 2

Ingredients:

- 14.5 oz can chickpeas, drained & rinsed
- 1/8 tsp ground ginger
- 1 tsp garlic powder
- 1 tsp ground coriander
- 1 tsp ground cumin
- 2 tsp olive oil

Directions:

1. In a mixing bowl, add chickpeas, ginger, garlic powder, coriander, cumin, and oil and mix well.
2. Place the cooking pot in the unit then place the crisper basket in the pot.
3. Select air crisp mode set the temperature to 370 F and set the time to 20 minutes. Press start to begin preheating.
4. Once the unit is preheated then spread chickpeas in the crisper basket. Close with a lid and cook. Stir chickpeas halfway through.
5. Serve and enjoy.

Nutritional Value (Amount per Serving):

- Calories 294
- Fat 7.3 g
- Carbohydrates 48 g
- Sugar 0.4 g
- Protein 10.6 g
- Cholesterol 0 mg

Sausage Meatballs

Preparation Time: 10 minutes
Cooking Time: 10 minutes
Serve: 4

Ingredients:

- 1 egg, lightly beaten
- 1 lb pork sausage
- 1/2 tbsp fresh rosemary, minced
- 2 tbsp fresh parsley, minced
- 2 tbsp breadcrumbs
- 2 oz pimientos, diced
- 1/2 tsp curry powder
- 1 tsp garlic, minced
- 1 tbsp olive oil
- Pepper
- Salt

Directions:

1. Add all ingredients into the mixing bowl and mix until well combined.
2. Make 1-1/4-inch balls from the meat mixture.
3. Place the cooking pot in the unit then place the crisper basket in the pot.
4. Select air crisp mode set the temperature to 400 F and set the time to 10 minutes. Press start to begin preheating.
5. Once the unit is preheated then place meatballs in the crisper basket. Close with a lid and cook for 10 minutes.
6. Serve and enjoy.

Nutritional Value (Amount per Serving):

- Calories 466
- Fat 37.2 g
- Carbohydrates 7.8 g
- Sugar 3.3 g
- Protein 24.6 g
- Cholesterol 136 mg

Easy Squash Fries

Preparation Time: 10 minutes
Cooking Time: 12 minutes
Serve: 2

Ingredients:

- 1/2 lb delicate squash
- Pepper
- Salt

Directions:

1. Scoop out the seeds & cut the squash into the fries shape.
2. In a bowl, toss squash fries with pepper and salt.
3. Place the cooking pot in the unit then place the crisper basket in the pot.
4. Select air crisp mode set the temperature to 390 F and set the time to 12 minutes. Press start to begin preheating.
5. Once the unit is preheated then place squash fries in the crisper basket. Close with a lid and cook for 12 minutes. Turn fries halfway through.
6. Serve and enjoy.

Nutritional Value (Amount per Serving):

- Calories 40
- Fat 0 g
- Carbohydrates 0 g
- Sugar 4 g
- Protein 1.4 g
- Cholesterol 0 mg

Stuffed Jalapenos

Preparation Time: 10 minutes
Cooking Time: 15 minutes
Serve: 4

Ingredients:

- 1/2 lb jalapenos, halved & seeded
- 1/4 cup breadcrumbs
- 1/8 tsp paprika
- 1/8 tsp chili powder
- 1/8 tsp garlic powder
- 3 bacon slices, cooked & crumbled
- 6 tbsp Monterey jack cheese, shredded
- 6 tbsp cheddar cheese, shredded
- 4 oz cream cheese, softened
- 1/8 tsp salt

Directions:

1. In a bowl, mix cream cheese, cheddar cheese, Monterey jack cheese, bacon, garlic powder, chili powder, paprika, breadcrumbs, and salt.
2. Stuff cream cheese mixture into each jalapeno half.
3. Place the cooking pot in the unit then place the crisper basket in the pot.
4. Select air crisp mode set the temperature to 325 F and set the time to 15 minutes. Press start to begin preheating.
5. Once the unit is preheated then place stuffed peppers in the crisper basket. Close with a lid and cook for 15 minutes.
6. Serve and enjoy.

Nutritional Value (Amount per Serving):

- Calories 303
- Fat 23.3 g
- Carbohydrates 9.5 g
- Sugar 2.6 g
- Protein 14.4 g
- Cholesterol 67 mg

Roasted Nuts

Preparation Time: 10 minutes
Cooking Time: 20 minutes
Serve: 4

Ingredients:

- 2 cups mixed nuts
- 1/2 tsp paprika
- 1 tbsp sugar
- 1 tsp cinnamon
- 2 tbsp egg white

Directions:

1. In a bowl, add mixed nuts, paprika, sugar, cinnamon, and egg white and mix well.
2. Place the cooking pot in the unit then place the crisper basket in the pot.
3. Select air crisp mode set the temperature to 300 F and set the time to 20 minutes. Press start to begin preheating.
4. Once the unit is preheated then place mixed nuts in the crisper basket. Close with a lid and cook for 20 minutes. Stir nuts halfway through.
5. Serve and enjoy.

Nutritional Value (Amount per Serving):

- Calories 460
- Fat 40.5 g
- Carbohydrates 19.7 g
- Sugar 6.2 g
- Protein 12.1 g
- Cholesterol 0 mg

Healthy Yuca Fries

Preparation Time: 10 minutes
Cooking Time: 15 minutes
Serve: 2

Ingredients:

- 1 lb yuca, peeled & cut into fries shape
- 1 tbsp dried parsley
- 1/2 tsp garlic powder
- 1/4 cup olive oil
- 1 tsp dried oregano
- 1/2 tsp paprika
- 1/2 tsp salt

Directions:

1. Boil yuca fries in 2 cups of water for 5 minutes. Drain well and pat dry and transfer in a large bowl.
2. Add remaining ingredients into the bowl and mix well.
3. Place the cooking pot in the unit then place the crisper basket in the pot.
4. Select air crisp mode set the temperature to 380 F and set the time to 15 minutes. Press start to begin preheating.
5. Once the unit is preheated then place yucca fries in the crisper basket. Close with a lid and cook for 15 minutes.
6. Serve and enjoy.

Nutritional Value (Amount per Serving):

- Calories 495
- Fat 25.4 g
- Carbohydrates 62.7 g
- Sugar 0.3 g
- Protein 7.1 g
- Cholesterol 0 mg

Delicious Chicken Patties

Preparation Time: 10 minutes
Cooking Time: 12 minutes
Serve: 4

Ingredients:

- 1 lb ground chicken
- 1/2 tsp Italian seasoning
- 1/2 tsp garlic powder
- 1 tsp onion powder
- 1 tbsp parsley, chopped
- 1/2 cup parmesan cheese, grated
- 1/4 cup Greek yogurt
- 1/2 tsp salt

Directions:

1. Add all ingredients into the mixing bowl and mix until well combined.
2. Make small patties from the meat mixture.
3. Place the cooking pot in the unit then place the crisper basket in the pot.
4. Select air crisp mode set the temperature to 400 F and set the time to 12 minutes. Press start to begin preheating.
5. Once the unit is preheated then place patties in the crisper basket. Close with a lid and cook for 12 minutes. Flip patties halfway through.
6. Serve and enjoy.

Nutritional Value (Amount per Serving):

- Calories 266
- Fat 11.3 g
- Carbohydrates 1.8 g
- Sugar 0.9 g
- Protein 37.8 g
- Cholesterol 110 mg

Easy Sausage Balls

Preparation Time: 10 minute
Cooking Time: 18 minutes
Serve: 4

Ingredients:

- 1 lb ground pork sausage
- 1 cup cheddar cheese, shredded
- 1 cup almond flour
- Pepper
- Salt

Directions:

1. Add all ingredients into the mixing bowl and mix until well combined.
2. Make meatballs from meat mixture.
3. Place the cooking pot in the unit then place the crisper basket in the pot.
4. Select air crisp mode set the temperature to 375 F and set the time to 18 minutes. Press start to begin preheating.
5. Once the unit is preheated then place meatballs in the crisper basket. Close with a lid and cook for 18 minutes. Flip sausage balls halfway through.
6. Serve and enjoy.

Nutritional Value (Amount per Serving):

- Calories 514
- Fat 42.9 g
- Carbohydrates 1.9 g
- Sugar 0.4 g
- Protein 28.5 g
- Cholesterol 130 mg

Flavorful Tofu Bites

Preparation Time: 10 minutes
Cooking Time: 13 minutes
Serve: 4

Ingredients:

- 12 oz extra-firm tofu block, cut into 1/2-inch cubes
- 1/2 tsp pepper
- 1 tsp garlic powder
- 1 tsp onion powder
- 1 tsp paprika
- 2 tsp cornstarch
- 1 tbsp olive oil
- 1/2 tsp salt

Directions:

1. Add tofu and remaining ingredients into the mixing bowl and toss well to coat.
2. Place the cooking pot in the unit then place the crisper basket in the pot.
3. Select air crisp mode set the temperature to 390 F and set the time to 13 minutes. Press start to begin preheating.
4. Once the unit is preheated then place tofu cubes in the crisper basket. Close with a lid and cook for 13 minutes. Stir tofu pieces halfway through.
5. Serve and enjoy.

Nutritional Value (Amount per Serving):

- Calories 85
- Fat 5.2 g
- Carbohydrates 3.8 g
- Sugar 0.4 g
- Protein 7.9 g
- Cholesterol 0 mg

Healthy Carrot Fries

Preparation Time: 10 minutes
Cooking Time: 15 minutes
Serve: 4

Ingredients:

- 2 carrots, peeled and cut into fries
- 1/4 tsp garlic powder
- 1 tbsp olive oil
- 1 tbsp parmesan cheese, grated
- Pepper
- Salt

Directions:

1. Add carrots and remaining ingredients into the bowl and toss well.
2. Place the cooking pot in the unit then place the crisper basket in the pot.
3. Select air crisp mode set the temperature to 350 F and set the time to 15 minutes. Press start to begin preheating.
4. Once the unit is preheated then place carrot fries in the crisper basket. Close with a lid and cook for 15 minutes. Stir halfway through.
5. Serve and enjoy.

Nutritional Value (Amount per Serving):

- Calories 53
- Fat 4.1 g
- Carbohydrates 3.3 g
- Sugar 1.5 g
- Protein 1.2 g
- Cholesterol 2 mg

Tasty Potato Nuggets

Preparation Time: 10 minutes
Cooking Time: 12 minutes
Serve: 4

Ingredients:

- 2 cups potatoes, diced
- 4 cups kale, chopped
- ½ tsp garlic, minced
- 1 tsp olive oil
- 2 tbsp milk
- Pepper
- Salt

Directions:

1. Add 5 cups of water in a stockpot and bring to boil. Add potatoes and cook until tender. Drain well.
2. Heat oil in a pan over medium-high heat.
3. Add kale and cook for 3 minutes. Add garlic and stir for 30 seconds.
4. Transfer kale in a bowl.
5. Add potatoes, milk, pepper, and salt and mash potato using a fork and stir to combine.
6. Make small nuggets from potato mixture.
7. Place the cooking pot in the unit then place the crisper basket in the pot.
8. Select air crisp mode set the temperature to 390 F and set the time to 12 minutes. Press start to begin preheating.
9. Once the unit is preheated then place potato nuggets in the crisper basket. Close with a lid and cook for 12 minutes.
10. Serve and enjoy.

Nutritional Value (Amount per Serving):

- Calories 100
- Fat 1.4 g
- Carbohydrates 19.4 g
- Sugar 1.2 g
- Protein 3.6 g
- Cholesterol 1 mg

Cinnamon Sweet Potato Bites

Preparation Time: 10 minutes
Cooking Time: 25 minutes
Serve: 4

Ingredients:

- 3 medium sweet potatoes, peel and diced into cubes
- 2 tbsp honey
- 1 tbsp olive oil
- 2 tsp cinnamon

Directions:

1. Add sweet potatoes into the mixing bowl.
2. Add remaining ingredients over sweet potatoes and toss well.
3. Place the cooking pot in the unit then place the crisper basket in the pot.
4. Select air crisp mode set the temperature to 400 F and set the time to 25 minutes. Press start to begin preheating.
5. Once the unit is preheated then place sweet potatoes in the crisper basket. Close with a lid and cook for 25 minutes. Stir halfway through.
6. Serve and enjoy.

Nutritional Value (Amount per Serving):

- Calories 198
- Fat 3.7 g
- Carbohydrates 41 g
- Sugar 9.2 g
- Protein 1.8 g
- Cholesterol 0 mg

Spicy Peanuts

Preparation Time: 10 minutes
Cooking Time: 20 minutes
Serve: 4

Ingredients:

- 4 oz peanuts
- 1 1/2 tsp Old Bay seasoning
- 1 tbsp olive oil
- 1/2 tsp Cayenne pepper
- Salt

Directions:

1. In a mixing bowl, mix together cayenne pepper, old bay seasoning, olive oil, and salt. Add peanuts and stir until well coated.
2. Place the cooking pot in the unit then place the crisper basket in the pot.
3. Select air crisp mode set the temperature to 320 F and set the time to 20 minutes. Press start to begin preheating.
4. Once the unit is preheated then place peanuts in the crisper basket. Close with a lid and cook for 20 minutes. Stir halfway through.
5. Serve and enjoy.

Nutritional Value (Amount per Serving):

- Calories 191
- Fat 17.5 g
- Carbohydrates 4.7 g
- Sugar 1.2 g
- Protein 7.3 g
- Cholesterol 0 mg

Savory Cashew Nuts

Preparation Time: 10 minutes
Cooking Time: 5 minutes
Serve: 6

Ingredients:

- 3 cups cashews
- 1 tsp ground coriander
- 1 tsp paprika
- 2 tbsp olive oil
- 1 tsp ground cumin
- Salt

Directions:

1. Add cashews and remaining ingredients into the large bowl and toss well.
2. Place the cooking pot in the unit then place the crisper basket in the pot.
3. Select air crisp mode set the temperature to 330 F and set the time to 5 minutes. Press start to begin preheating.
4. Once the unit is preheated then place cashews in the crisper basket. Close with a lid and cook for 5 minutes.
5. Serve and enjoy.

Nutritional Value (Amount per Serving):

- Calories 436
- Fat 36.6 g
- Carbohydrates 22.7 g
- Sugar 3.5 g
- Protein 10.6 g
- Cholesterol 0 mg

Chapter 8: Dehydrate

Mango Slices

Preparation Time: 10 minutes
Cooking Time: 12 hours
Serve: 2

Ingredients:

- 2 mangoes, peel and cut into 1/4-inch thick slices
- 1/2 tbsp honey
- 2 tbsp lemon juice

Directions:

1. In a bowl, mix together lemon juice and honey. Add mango slices and coat well.
2. Place the cooking pot in the unit then place the crisper basket in the pot.
3. Arrange mango slices in the crisper basket.
4. Select dehydrate mode, set temperature to 135 F, and set the time to 12 hours. Close with a lid and press start.
5. Serve and enjoy.

Nutritional Value (Amount per Serving):

- Calories 221
- Fat 1.4 g
- Carbohydrates 55 g
- Sugar 50.5 g
- Protein 2.9 g
- Cholesterol 0 mg

Green Apple Chips

Preparation Time: 10 minutes
Cooking Time: 8 hours
Serve: 2

Ingredients:

- 2 green apples, cored and sliced 1/8 inch thick
- 1 tbsp lime juice

Directions:

1. Add apple slices and lime juice in a bowl and toss well and set aside for 10 minutes.
2. Place the cooking pot in the unit then place the crisper basket in the pot.
3. Arrange apple slices in the crisper basket.
4. Select dehydrate mode, set temperature to 145 F, and set the time to 8 hours. Close with a lid and press start.
5. Serve and enjoy.

Nutritional Value (Amount per Serving):

- Calories 122
- Fat 0.4 g
- Carbohydrates 32.7 g
- Sugar 23.6 g
- Protein 0.7 g
- Cholesterol 0 mg

Dried Raspberries

Preparation Time: 10 minutes
Cooking Time: 12 hours
Serve: 2

Ingredients:

- 2 cups raspberries, wash and dry
- 2 tbsp lemon juice

Directions:

1. Add raspberries and lemon juice in a bowl and toss well.
2. Place the cooking pot in the unit then place the crisper basket in the pot.
3. Arrange raspberries in the crisper basket.
4. Select dehydrate mode, set temperature to 135 F, and set the time to 12 hours. Close with a lid and press start.
5. Serve and enjoy.

Nutritional Value (Amount per Serving):

- Calories 68
- Fat 0.9 g
- Carbohydrates 15 g
- Sugar 5.8 g
- Protein 1.6 g
- Cholesterol 0 mg

Avocado Chips

Preparation Time: 10 minutes
Cooking Time: 10 hours
Serve: 2

Ingredients:

- 2 avocados, halved, pitted, & Cut into slices.
- 1 tbsp lemon juice
- 1/4 tsp cayenne pepper
- Salt

Directions:

1. Drizzle lemon juice over avocado slices and sprinkle with cayenne pepper and salt.
2. Place the cooking pot in the unit then place the crisper basket in the pot.
3. Arrange avocado slices in the crisper basket.
4. Select dehydrate mode, set temperature to 160 F, and set the time to 10 hours. Close with a lid and press start.
5. Serve and enjoy.

Nutritional Value (Amount per Serving):

- Calories 413
- Fat 39.3 g
- Carbohydrates 17.6 g
- Sugar 1.2 g
- Protein 3.9 g
- Cholesterol 0 mg

Strawberry Chips

Preparation Time: 10 minutes
Cooking Time: 12 hours
Serve: 3

Ingredients:

- 1 cup strawberries, cut into 1/8-inch thick slices

Directions:

1. Place the cooking pot in the unit then place the crisper basket in the pot.
2. Arrange strawberry slices in the crisper basket.
3. Select dehydrate mode, set temperature to 130 F, and set the time to 12 minutes. Close with a lid and press start.
4. Serve and enjoy.

Nutritional Value (Amount per Serving):

- Calories 15
- Fat 0.1 g
- Carbohydrates 3.7 g
- Sugar 2.4 g
- Protein 0.3 g
- Cholesterol 0 mg

Sweet Potato Chips

Preparation Time: 10 minutes
Cooking Time: 12 hours
Serve: 3

Ingredients:

- 1 sweet potato, sliced thinly
- 3 tbsp olive oil
- 1/2 tsp chili powder
- 1 tbsp cumin
- 1 tsp salt

Directions:

1. Add sweet potato slices into the large bowl. Mix together chili powder, cumin, oil, and salt and pour over sweet potato slices and toss well.
2. Place the cooking pot in the unit then place the crisper basket in the pot.
3. Arrange sweet potato slices in the crisper basket.
4. Select dehydrate mode, set temperature to 125 F, and set the time to 12 hours. Close with a lid and press start.
5. Serve and enjoy.

Nutritional Value (Amount per Serving):

- Calories 163
- Fat 14.6 g
- Carbohydrates 9 g
- Sugar 2.6 g
- Protein 1.2 g
- Cholesterol 0 mg

Cucumber Chips

Preparation Time: 10 minutes
Cooking Time: 12 hours
Serve: 2

Ingredients:

- 1 cucumber, sliced
- 1 tsp olive oil
- Salt

Directions:

1. In a bowl, toss cucumber slices with oil, and salt.
2. Place the cooking pot in the unit then place the crisper basket in the pot.
3. Arrange cucumber slices in the crisper basket.
4. Select dehydrate mode, set temperature to 135 F, and set the time to 12 hours. Close with a lid and press start.
5. Serve and enjoy.

Nutritional Value (Amount per Serving):

- Calories 44
- Fat 2.5 g
- Carbohydrates 5.7 g
- Sugar 2.5 g
- Protein 1.1 g
- Cholesterol 0 mg

Beet Chips

Preparation Time: 10 minutes
Cooking Time: 10 hours
Serve: 2

Ingredients:

- 1 medium beet, sliced thinly
- Sea salt

Directions:

1. Place the cooking pot in the unit then place the crisper basket in the pot.
2. Arrange beet slices in the crisper basket.
3. Select dehydrate mode, set temperature to 135 F, and set the time to 10 hours. Close with a lid and press start.
4. Serve and enjoy.

Nutritional Value (Amount per Serving):

- Calories 22
- Fat 0.1 g
- Carbohydrates 5 g
- Sugar 4 g
- Protein 0.8 g
- Cholesterol 0 mg

Carrot Chips

Preparation Time: 10 minutes
Cooking Time: 10 hours
Serve: 3

Ingredients:

- 2 carrots, peel and thinly sliced
- 1 tsp fresh lemon juice
- Salt

Directions:

1. In a bowl, add carrots, lemon juice, and salt and toss well.
2. Place the cooking pot in the unit then place the crisper basket in the pot.
3. Arrange carrot slices in the crisper basket.
4. Select dehydrate mode, set temperature to 115 F, and set the time to 10 hours. Close with a lid and press start.
5. Serve and enjoy.

Nutritional Value (Amount per Serving):

- Calories 18
- Fat 0 g
- Carbohydrates 4.2 g
- Sugar 2 g
- Protein 0.4 g
- Cholesterol 0 mg

Dehydrated Pineapple

Preparation Time: 10 minutes
Cooking Time: 12 hours
Serve: 3

Ingredients:

- 6 pineapple slices, 1/4-inch thick

Directions:

1. Place the cooking pot in the unit then place the crisper basket in the pot.
2. Arrange pineapple slices in the crisper basket.
3. Select dehydrate mode, set temperature to 135 F, and set the time to 12 hours. Close with a lid and press start.
4. Serve and enjoy.

Nutritional Value (Amount per Serving):

- Calories 133
- Fat 1.3 g
- Carbohydrates 19.3 g
- Sugar 16.7 g
- Protein 2 g
- Cholesterol 0 mg

Orange Chips

Preparation Time: 10 minutes
Cooking Time: 12 hours
Serve: 2

Ingredients:

- 2 oranges, seedless, peel, and cut into slices

Directions:

1. Place the cooking pot in the unit then place the crisper basket in the pot.
2. Arrange orange slices in the crisper basket.
3. Select dehydrate mode, set temperature to 135 F, and set the time to 12 hours. Close with a lid and press start.
4. Serve and enjoy.

Nutritional Value (Amount per Serving):

- Calories 58
- Fat 0.2 g
- Carbohydrates 14.4 g
- Sugar 11.5 g
- Protein 1.2 g
- Cholesterol 0 mg

Kiwi Chips

Preparation Time: 10 minutes
Cooking Time: 12 hours
Serve: 4

Ingredients:

- 3 kiwis, peel and cut into 1/4-inch thick slices

Directions:

1. Place the cooking pot in the unit then place the crisper basket in the pot.
2. Arrange kiwi slices in the crisper basket.
3. Select dehydrate mode, set temperature to 135 F, and set the time to 12 hours. Close with a lid and press start.
4. Serve and enjoy.

Nutritional Value (Amount per Serving):

- Calories 15
- Fat 1.2 g
- Carbohydrates 1 g
- Sugar 0.5 g
- Protein 0.3 g
- Cholesterol 0 mg

Apple Chips

Preparation Time: 10 minutes
Cooking Time: 8 hours
Serve: 4

Ingredients:

- 2 apples, cut into 1/8-inch thick slices
- 1 tsp cinnamon

Directions:

1. Place the cooking pot in the unit then place the crisper basket in the pot.
2. Arrange apple slices in the crisper basket and sprinkle with cinnamon.
3. Select dehydrate mode, set temperature to 135 F, and set the time to 8 hours. Close with a lid and press start.
4. Serve and enjoy.

Nutritional Value (Amount per Serving):

- Calories 59
- Fat 0.2 g
- Carbohydrates 15.9 g
- Sugar 11.6 g
- Protein 0.3 g
- Cholesterol 0 mg

Eggplant Slices

Preparation Time: 10 minutes
Cooking Time: 6 hours
Serve: 2

Ingredients:

- 1 medium eggplant, sliced 1/4-inch thick
- 1 1/2 tsp paprika
- 1/4 tsp onion powder
- 1/4 tsp garlic powder

Directions:

1. Add eggplant slices, onion powder, garlic powder, and paprika into the mixing bowl and toss well.
2. Place the cooking pot in the unit then place the crisper basket in the pot.
3. Arrange eggplant slices in the crisper basket.
4. Select dehydrate mode, set temperature to 140 F, and set the time to 6 hours. Close with a lid and press start.
5. Serve and enjoy.

Nutritional Value (Amount per Serving):

- Calories 64
- Fat 0.6 g
- Carbohydrates 14.8 g
- Sugar 7.2 g
- Protein 2.6 g
- Cholesterol 0 mg

Squash Chips

Preparation Time: 10 minutes
Cooking Time: 12 hours
Serve: 8

Ingredients:

- 2 cups yellow squash, sliced 1/8-inch thick
- 2 tsp olive oil
- 2 tbsp vinegar
- Salt

Directions:

1. Add squash slices into the large bowl.
2. Add vinegar, oil, and salt over squash slices and toss well.
3. Place the cooking pot in the unit then place the crisper basket in the pot.
4. Arrange yellow squash in the crisper basket.
5. Select dehydrate mode, set temperature to 110 F, and set the time to 12 hours. Close with a lid and press start.
6. Serve and enjoy.

Nutritional Value (Amount per Serving):

- Calories 15
- Fat 1.2 g
- Carbohydrates 1 g
- Sugar 0.5 g
- Protein 0.3 g
- Cholesterol 0 mg

Chapter 9: Desserts

Spiced Apples

Preparation Time: 10 minutes
Cooking Time: 10 minutes
Serve: 6

Ingredients:

- 4 apples, sliced
- 1 tsp apple pie spice
- 1/2 cup erythritol
- 2 tbsp butter, melted

Directions:

1. Add apple slices in a large bowl and sprinkle with sweetener and apple pie spice.
2. Add melted butter and toss to coat.
3. Transfer apple slices in a baking dish.
4. Place the cooking pot in the unit.
5. Select bake mode set the temperature to 350 F and set the time to 10 minutes. Press start to begin preheating.
6. Once the unit is preheated then place the baking dish in the cooking pot. Close with a lid and cook.
7. Serve and enjoy.

Nutritional Value (Amount per Serving):

- Calories 73
- Fat 4.6 g
- Carbohydrates 8.2 g
- Sugar 5.4 g
- Protein 0 g
- Cholesterol 0 mg

Blueberry Muffins

Preparation Time: 10 minutes
Cooking Time: 20 minutes
Serve: 12

Ingredients:

- 3 large eggs
- 1/3 cup milk
- 1/3 cup coconut oil, melted
- 1 1/2 tsp baking powder
- 1/2 cup erythritol
- 2 1/2 cups almond flour
- 3/4 cup blueberries
- 1/2 tsp vanilla

Directions:

1. In a large bowl, mix together almond flour, baking powder, erythritol.
2. Stir in the coconut oil, vanilla, eggs, and milk. Add blueberries and fold well.
3. Pour batter into the silicone muffin molds.
4. Place the cooking pot in the unit.
5. Select bake mode set the temperature to 325 F and set the time to 20 minutes. Press start to begin preheating.
6. Once the unit is preheated then place muffin molds in the cooking pot. Close with a lid and cook.
7. Serve and enjoy.

Nutritional Value (Amount per Serving):

- Calories 215
- Fat 19 g
- Carbohydrates 5 g
- Sugar 2 g
- Protein 7 g
- Cholesterol 45 mg

Pound Cake

Preparation Time: 10 minutes
Cooking Time: 35 minutes
Serve: 9

Ingredients:

- 5 eggs
- 1/2 cup butter, softened
- 1 tsp baking powder
- 7 oz almond flour
- 1 tsp vanilla
- 1 tsp orange extract
- 1 cup Splenda
- 4 oz cream cheese, softened

Directions:

1. Add all ingredients into the mixing bowl and mix until the batter is fluffy.
2. Pour batter into the greased baking dish.
3. Place the cooking pot in the unit.
4. Select bake mode set the temperature to 350 F and set the time to 35 minutes. Press start to begin preheating.
5. Once the unit is preheated then place the baking dish in the cooking pot. Close with a lid and cook.
6. Slices and serve.

Nutritional Value (Amount per Serving):

- Calories 287
- Fat 27.2 g
- Carbohydrates 5.2 g
- Sugar 1 g
- Protein 8.5 g
- Cholesterol 132 mg

Choco Almond Muffins

Preparation Time: 10 minutes
Cooking Time: 30 minutes
Serve: 8

Ingredients:

- 2 eggs
- 1/2 cup cream
- 1 tsp vanilla extract
- 4 tbsp Swerve
- 1/2 cup cocoa powder
- 1 cup ground almonds

Directions:

1. In a bowl, mix together all dry ingredients.
2. In another bowl, beat together eggs, vanilla, and cream.
3. Pour egg mixture into the dry ingredients and mix well to combine.
4. Pour batter into the silicone muffin molds.
5. Place the cooking pot in the unit.
6. Select bake mode set the temperature to 375 F and set the time to 30 minutes. Press start to begin preheating.
7. Once the unit is preheated then place muffin molds in the cooking pot. Close with a lid and cook.
8. Serve and enjoy.

Nutritional Value (Amount per Serving):

- Calories 86
- Fat 6.9 g
- Carbohydrates 9.7 g
- Protein 4 g
- Sugar 0.8 g
- Cholesterol 35mg

Moist Brownies

Preparation Time: 10 minutes
Cooking Time: 40 minutes
Serve: 8

Ingredients:

- 1/4 cup walnuts, chopped
- 1/2 cup butter, melted
- 1/2 cup chocolate chips
- 2 tsp vanilla
- 1 tbsp milk
- 3/4 cup yogurt
- 1 cup all-purpose flour
- 1/3 cup cocoa powder
- 2 tsp baking powder
- 1 cup of sugar
- 1/4 tsp salt

Directions:

1. In a bowl, mix flour, baking powder, cocoa powder, and salt. Set aside.
2. In another bowl, add butter, vanilla, milk, and yogurt and stir until combined.
3. Add flour mixture into the butter mixture and mix until just combined. Fold in walnuts and chocolate chips.
4. Pour batter into the greased baking dish.
5. Place the cooking pot in the unit.
6. Select bake mode set the temperature to 350 F and set the time to 40 minutes. Press start to begin preheating.
7. Once the unit is preheated then place the baking dish in the cooking pot. Close with a lid and cook.
8. Slice and serve.

Nutritional Value (Amount per Serving):

- Calories 362
- Fat 17.9 g
- Carbohydrates 48 g
- Sugar 32.4 g
- Protein 5.5 g
- Cholesterol 34 mg

Easy Butter Cake

Preparation Time: 10 minutes
Cooking Time: 30 minutes
Serve: 8

Ingredients:

- 1 egg, beaten
- 1 cup all-purpose flour
- 1/2 tsp vanilla
- 3/4 cup sugar
- 1/2 cup butter, softened

Directions:

1. In a mixing bowl, mix together sugar and butter.
2. Add egg, flour, and vanilla and mix until combined.
3. Pour batter into greased baking dish.
4. Place the cooking pot in the unit.
5. Select bake mode set the temperature to 350 F and set the time to 30 minutes. Press start to begin preheating.
6. Once the unit is preheated then place the baking dish in the cooking pot. Close with a lid and cook.
7. Slice and serve.

Nutritional Value (Amount per Serving):

- Calories 211
- Fat 10.9 g
- Carbohydrates 27.4 g
- Sugar 16.8 g
- Protein 2.2 g
- Cholesterol 45 mg

Baked Donuts

Preparation Time: 10 minutes
Cooking Time: 15 minutes
Serve: 8

Ingredients:

- 2 eggs
- 1 cup almond flour
- 1/4 tsp baking soda
- 1 1/2 tsp vanilla extract
- 3 tbsp maple syrup

Directions:

1. In a large bowl, add all ingredients and mix well until smooth.
2. Pour batter into the silicone donut molds.
3. Place the cooking pot in the unit.
4. Select bake mode set the temperature to 320 F and set the time to 15 minutes. Press start to begin preheating.
5. Once the unit is preheated then place donut molds in the cooking pot. Close with a lid and cook.
6. Serve and enjoy.

Nutritional Value (Amount per Serving):

- Calories 122
- Fat 7.8 g
- Carbohydrates 8.2 g
- Protein 4.4 g
- Sugars 4.6 g
- Cholesterol 41 mg

Peanut Butter Muffins

Preparation Time: 10 minutes
Cooking Time: 20 minutes
Serve: 12

Ingredients:

- 1 cup peanut butter
- 1 cup applesauce
- 1 tsp baking soda
- 1 tsp vanilla
- 1/2 cup maple syrup
- 1/2 cup cocoa powder

Directions:

1. Add all ingredients into the blender and blend until smooth.
2. Pour blended mixture into silicone muffin molds.
3. Place the cooking pot in the unit.
4. Select bake mode set the temperature to 350 F and set the time to 20 minutes. Press start to begin preheating.
5. Once the unit is preheated then place muffin molds in the cooking pot. Close with a lid and cook.
6. Serve and enjoy.

Nutritional Value (Amount per Serving):

- Calories 178
- Fat 11.3 g
- Carbohydrates 17.3 g
- Sugar 12 g
- Protein 6.1 g
- Cholesterol 0 mg

Strawberry Cobbler

Preparation Time: 10 minutes
Cooking Time: 45 minutes
Serve: 6

Ingredients:

- 2 cups strawberries, diced
- 1 cup milk
- 1 1/4 cup sugar
- 1 tsp vanilla
- 1 cup self-rising flour
- 1/2 cup butter, melted

Directions:

1. In a bowl, mix flour and 1 cup sugar.
2. Add milk and whisk until smooth.
3. Add vanilla and butter and mix well.
4. Pour mixture into the greased baking dish and sprinkle with strawberries and top with remaining sugar.
5. Place the cooking pot in the unit.
6. Select bake mode set the temperature to 350 F and set the time to 45 minutes. Press start to begin preheating.
7. Once the unit is preheated then place the baking dish in the cooking pot. Close with a lid and cook.
8. Serve and enjoy.

Nutritional Value (Amount per Serving):

- Calories 405
- Fat 16.5 g
- Carbohydrates 63.4 g
- Sugar 46 g
- Protein 4 g
- Cholesterol 44 mg

Lemon Muffins

Preparation Time: 10 minutes
Cooking Time: 15 minutes
Serve: 12

Ingredients:

- 2 eggs
- 1/3 cup butter, melted
- 1/3 cup swerve
- 1 fresh lemon juice
- 1/2 cup yogurt
- 1 tsp baking powder
- 1 1/4 cup almond flour
- 1 tbsp lemon zest

Directions:

1. Add all ingredients into the mixing bowl and mix until well combined.
2. Pour batter into the silicone muffin molds.
3. Place the cooking pot in the unit.
4. Select bake mode set the temperature to 350 F and set the time to 15 minutes. Press start to begin preheating.
5. Once the unit is preheated then place muffin molds in the cooking pot. Close with a lid and cook.
6. Serve and enjoy.

Nutritional Value (Amount per Serving):

- Calories 135
- Fat 11.5 g
- Carbohydrates 3.7 g
- Sugar 0.9 g
- Protein 4.1 g
- Cholesterol 41 mg

Chapter 10: 30-Day Meal Plan

Day 1

Breakfast- Delicious Baked Oatmeal

Lunch-Marinated Grill Chicken

Dinner- Juicy Pork Chops

Day 2

Breakfast- Broccoli Cauliflower Bake

Lunch-Juicy Chicken Thighs

Dinner-Flavorful Honey Pork Chops

Day 3

Breakfast- Scalloped Potatoes

Lunch-Grill Greek Chicken

Dinner-Herb Pork Chops

Day 4

Breakfast- Zucchini Casserole

Lunch-Spicy Chicken Wings

Dinner-Crispy Pork Chops

Day 5

Breakfast- Cheese Egg Bake

Lunch-Grilled Chicken Breast

Dinner-Mexican Steak

Day 6

Breakfast- Crispy Breakfast Potatoes

Lunch-Baked Chicken Breast

Dinner-Asian Lamb Chops

Day 7

Breakfast- Greek Egg Muffins

Lunch-Crunchy Chicken Tenders

Dinner-Tuscan Steak

Day 8

Breakfast- Greek Egg Muffins

Lunch-Ranch Chicken Wings

Dinner- Creole Lamb Chops

Day 9

Breakfast- Spinach Frittata

Lunch-Easy Jerk Chicken Wings

Dinner-Marinated Pork Chops

Day 10

Breakfast- Quinoa Egg Muffins

Lunch-Sweet & Spicy Chicken Wings

Dinner-Grilled Pork Chops

Day 11

Breakfast- Delicious Baked Oatmeal

Lunch-Cajun Fish Fillets

Dinner-Flavorful Southwest Chicken

Day 12

Breakfast- Broccoli Cauliflower Bake

Lunch-Dijon Salmon Fillets

Dinner-Garlic Mustard Chicken

Day 13

Breakfast- Scalloped Potatoes

Lunch-Blackened Cod

Dinner-Basil Thyme Chicken Breast

Day 14

Breakfast- Zucchini Casserole

Lunch-Lemon Garlic Salmon

Dinner-Asian Chicken Thighs

Day 15

Breakfast- Cheese Egg Bake

Lunch-Flavorful Mahi Mahi

Dinner-Herb Chicken Breast

Day 16

Breakfast- Delicious Baked Oatmeal

Lunch-Marinated Grill Chicken

Dinner- Juicy Pork Chops

Day 17

Breakfast- Broccoli Cauliflower Bake

Lunch-Juicy Chicken Thighs

Dinner-Flavorful Honey Pork Chops

Day 18

Breakfast- Scalloped Potatoes

Lunch-Grill Greek Chicken

Dinner-Herb Pork Chops

Day 19

Breakfast- Zucchini Casserole

Lunch-Spicy Chicken Wings

Dinner-Crispy Pork Chops

Day 20

Breakfast- Cheese Egg Bake

Lunch-Grilled Chicken Breast

Dinner-Mexican Steak

Day 21

Breakfast- Crispy Breakfast Potatoes

Lunch-Baked Chicken Breast

Dinner-Asian Lamb Chops

Day 22

Breakfast- Greek Egg Muffins

Lunch-Crunchy Chicken Tenders

Dinner-Tuscan Steak

Day 23

Breakfast- Greek Egg Muffins

Lunch-Ranch Chicken Wings

Dinner- Creole Lamb Chops

Day 24

Breakfast- Spinach Frittata

Lunch-Easy Jerk Chicken Wings

Dinner-Marinated Pork Chops

Day 25

Breakfast- Quinoa Egg Muffins

Lunch-Sweet & Spicy Chicken Wings

Dinner-Grilled Pork Chops

Day 26

Breakfast- Delicious Baked Oatmeal

Lunch-Cajun Fish Fillets

Dinner-Flavorful Southwest Chicken

Day 27

Breakfast- Broccoli Cauliflower Bake

Lunch-Dijon Salmon Fillets

Dinner-Garlic Mustard Chicken

Day 28

Breakfast- Scalloped Potatoes

Lunch-Blackened Cod

Dinner-Basil Thyme Chicken Breast

Day 29

Breakfast- Zucchini Casserole

Lunch-Lemon Garlic Salmon

Dinner-Asian Chicken Thighs

Day 30

Breakfast- Cheese Egg Bake

Lunch-Flavorful Mahi Mahi

Dinner-Herb Chicken Breast

Conclusion

Another revolutionary cooking appliance comes from Ninja Family is popularly known as Ninja Foodi Grill. These multifunctional cooking appliances not only grill your food but also air fry, roast, bake, and even dehydrate your favourite foods. The body of the appliances is made up of stainless steel and the upper domed lid is made from a plastic material. The accessories like grill grate, cooking pot, the crisper pot come with ceramic non-stick coating. It works on 1760 watts and produces a maximum 500°F to 510°F temperature while cooking your food.

This cookbook contains tasty, healthy, and delicious recipes that come from different categories like breakfast, poultry, beef, pork & lamb, fish & seafood, vegetable & side dishes, snacks & appetizers, dehydrate, and desserts. The recipes written in this book are unique and written in an easily understandable form. All the recipes are written with their preparation and cooking time with step by step cooking instructions. The recipes written in this book are ends with their nutritional value information.

www.ingramcontent.com/pod-product-compliance
Lightning Source LLC
Chambersburg PA
CBHW081346070526
44578CB00005B/745